DO NO HARM

DO NO HARM

SOCIAL SIN AND CHRISTIAN RESPONSIBILITY

STEPHEN G. RAY JR.

Fortress Press
Minneapolis

√

DO NO HARM
SOCIAL SIN AND CHRISTIAN RESPONSIBILITY

Scripture is from the Revised Standard Version of the Bible, copyright © 1946, 1952, 1971 by the Division of Christian Education of the National Council of the Churches of Christ in the USA. Used by permission.

Cover design: Brad Norr Design
Book design: Ann Delgehausen

Library of Congress Cataloging-in-Publication Data

Ray, Stephen G.
Do no harm : social sin and Christian responsibility / Stephen G. Ray, Jr.
    p. cm.
  Includes bibliographical references.
    ISBN 0-8006-3497-7 (pbk. : alk. paper)
    1. Sin—Social aspects—Terminology. 2. Protestant churches—
Doctrines—Terminology. 3. Language and languages—Religious
aspects—Christianity. I. Title.
BT715 .R39 2002
241'.3—dc21   2002013272

The paper used in this publication meets the minimum requirements of American National Standard for Information Sciences—Permanence of Paper for Printed Library Materials, ANSI Z329.48-1984.

Manufactured in the U.S.A.
07   06   05   04   03   1   2   3   4   5   6   7   8   9   10

My appreciation for the love and support I have received from my family is deep. Their care and kindness have made me. It is to them that I dedicate this work. Susan and Kiara, my heart sings because of you.

CONTENTS

PREFACE

"Sticks and stones may break my bones, but names can never hurt me!" As any child who has ever fallen back on these words as a final line of defense knows, names do hurt. As any person who has hurled an epithet knows, names do maim. As everyone sadly knows, in the right circumstances names can kill. Names have the power to strip the protective aura of humanity from people and leave them vulnerable to all manner of ravages at the hands of their "neighbors." Names like *urban predator, welfare cheat, fag, dyke, nigger,* or *kike* have the power to signal to all that anyone to whom these names are applied is persona non grata in the public life and space of the society in which they live. Another name, often spoken in conjunction with these, has the power not only to extend the range of social exclusion, but also to give that marginalization divine sanction. That name? *Sinner!* This title not only baptizes the terms of a particular

person's or group's social ostracism, it can render support and participation in their oppression a moral responsibility. Names, especially names like these, are
neither toys nor quaint word games. They are serious
business because the consequences of their use can be
devastating to the lives and well-being of God's children.

The desolating power of the name *sinner* is one that
should be apparent to anyone even vaguely familiar with
Christian history. People have been ghettoized, exiled,
and killed because they have been designated sinners.
Whether it be flogging, dunking, quartering, or burning
at the stake, no punishment has been deemed too severe
by "good church folk" when it is visited upon sinners in
their midst. Thankfully, there have been episodes
throughout our history in which some Christians have
dissented from this "works-of-the-blade" righteousness,
and with their challenge altered the course of human history. Precisely because the church has held such an important place in the development of Western society—and
the world by virtue of Western society's global influence—
its naming of persons and communities has had the
power to legitimate or contest often murderous exclusion. This power has largely been expressed by designat-
ing who is a sinner and who is not. With the use of a
simple name, Christian communities have often held, lit-
erally, the power of life and death in their hands. The latter choice has too often been made. This book deals with
a series of questions about Christian sin-talk and its social ramifications: Why it is that when "good church
folks" talk about sin and sinners they seem so oblivious
to the consequences of their rhetoric? Is it by intent or

just malfeasance that practitioners of Christian sin-talk (lay, clergy, and professional alike) so often find their rhetoric participating in, if not downright morally supporting, the systems of exclusion and marginalization in their social and cultural contexts? Why has Christian sin-talk so often been, as Martin Luther King Jr. observed, the "taillights of culture" that only illuminated those left as roadkill in the paths of history, and only rarely the headlights that identified a less deadly route? In seeking to answer these questions, my hope is to do more than reinforce the parental dictum that "it's not nice to call people names." I want to help readers understand how even the best-intentioned sin-talk can participate in needless and, in many cases, malicious harm to marginalized persons and their communities.

Let me be clear: The type of harm this book deals with is not only the emotional harm caused by name-calling. It is about harm that takes the form of the lynch mob's rope, or the ethnic cleanser's camps. It is about the harm that deadens the human conscience to the needs of the poor, or saps the capacity for empathy in the face of a plague (AIDS). This book offers an analysis of several situations in which sin-talk does more harm than good. By identifying the snares that entangled several famously well-meaning theologians who grappled with social sin, my work offers insights for ways of talking about sin, particularly social sin, that ameliorate the suffering of the weak instead of exacerbating it. This is a book for anyone who believes that the Christian concept of sin is helpful for critiquing and engaging hurtful social practices. More importantly, it is for people who want to understand how sin-talk can be used as an incisive tool that cuts with the hope of healing, not just a tool that wounds.

In laying out the hopes I have for this work, I would be remiss if I did not offer words of thanks to those whose efforts fostered this project. Although space does not permit me to express my gratitude to them all, there are a number of persons to whom I owe a special debt. First, my deepest thanks go to my longtime conversation partner and friend of the mind Serene Jones. Without her insight and helpful criticism, what value there is in this book would certainly be diminished. I owe a huge debt of gratitude to the administration and my faculty colleagues at Louisville Presbyterian Theological Seminary. The support and encouragement that I received from this community during the completion of this book were amazing. I am grateful, as well, to my friend and colleague Charles Marsh for allowing me to share a portion of this work with the Project on Lived Theology's Race Workgroup. The comments I received from fellow workgroup participants were very helpful. Special thanks are extended to my friend and editor Kaudie McLean for her insight and wisdom, and to my colleague Dale Andrews for lending his ear to many last-minute revisions.

INTRODUCTION

The eye is the lamp of the body.
–Matt. 6:22

Any number of sage sayings point to the importance of the eyes as windows to the world. We do well to remember also that windows not only allow us to receive images of the world beyond ourselves, they permit us to gaze upon that world. So, what we see of the world is inextricably bound to the light that our gaze casts upon it. What we see in the actions of others and how we understand appropriate responses are both conditioned by the interpretive structure that helps us to make sense of, or see, reality. As we construe the doings of others–how we attribute motives, how we experience the effects of their actions, and how we prescribe consequences–we are inescapably affected by how we see those doings *and the doers.* The gaze that we cast upon the being and actions of others is very much influenced by the way we see those others in the first place. This is nowhere more true than when we gaze upon sin and sinners.

I begin this book about sin-talk by bringing attention to the eye because sin, and our discourse about it, has everything to do with how we see the world and one another. What we name as sin, how we respond to it, and the culpability that we ascribe to the sinner correlates strongly with the interpretive framework through which we see those persons and their actions. If we otherwise think well of certain sinners, their sin likely gets a different sort of scrutiny than does the sin of persons to whom we are less well disposed. So, for instance, in a bygone era in many parts of the United States someone with particularly unpleasant views about African Americans was referred to as just "old-fashioned," while someone who held to the views espoused by the Nation of Islam was referred to as a "rabid racist" or "dangerous Anti-Semite." In each case, the sin is the same—demeaning and dehumanizing God's children—yet, the discursive rendering of the sin, and its gravity, differs according to the vantage point of the observer. This is no small point because as I will demonstrate throughout this book, the behaviors of societies, peoples, and churches are conditioned by the types of assessments they make of sinners in their midst. There are very real systematic and material consequences to the way that sin and sinners are named.

These material consequences are the result of a mediating moment in the chain of cognitive and physical events that I have implicitly used above: seeing, naming, and acting. The mediating moment in this chain, naming, is the one

I am focusing on because it is the point at which sin-talk either facilitates the engagement with social sin, or goes awry with sometimes deadly consequences. By bringing attention to the importance of naming, I intend further to bring attention to its connection with seeing. Specifically, I will bring awareness to the reality that the very way we see the world, including sin and sinners, is structured by the common senses of our contexts and more often than not reinforce our social presumptions. This is not a problem when the common wisdom works for the public good (e.g., children should be in school and not factories). Common wisdom can be devastating, however, when it undergirds fundamentally unjust social relations (e.g., the poor bring their calamities upon themselves). It is just this type of instance we must be concerned about, especially when seemingly well-meaning sin-talk participates in it.

The literature of sin over the last ten years has broadly focused two projects. First, it has sought to remind contemporary audiences that sin abounds and that our society is paying the consequences. In this genre we have the rumblings of the more reactionary segments of the Christian community. Second, in more recent years, we have the works of liberation-minded people who argue forcefully for an interpretation of sin that critiques material social and economic relationships. What these projects share is a sense that sin, left unabated, has very real social consequences. While they may disagree on what it is that they mean by sin, or which sins bear greater scrutiny, they agree that attention must be paid to the social life of sin. What they miss is a recognition that along with the need to talk about sin in its social dimension there is a corollary necessity to notice *how* we talk about sin. It seems essential to me that theologians

recognize that the way they talk about the social consequences of sin may have consequences of its own. Put another way, careless sin-talk can cause at least as much harm
as it can good. My project, then, is to bring attention to the
need for theologians to "watch their mouths" as they speak
about sin as a social dilemma. I am not, therefore, challenging the need to speak about the social sources or consequences of sin. Rather, I am contending that a significant
dimension of that engagement must be attentiveness to the
effects that sin-talk may have in its particular contexts.

I will explore the ways in which several Protestant theologians define and describe the reality loosely referred to
as "social sin." More specifically, I will discuss the images,
figures, metaphors, examples, and other rhetorical gestures
they use when they depict the reality of social evil. My contention is that much of this social sin-talk is highly problematic because, in an effort to name social sin, theologians
often unwittingly describe it in terms that may themselves
be profoundly racist, sexist, heterosexist, anti-Semitic, and
classist. When this happens their theological accounts of sin
ironically reiterate (rather than contest) the discursive reasoning of the corrupted social systems against which they
are ostensibly raging. At the very moment they are trying to
reveal and contest the roots of social sin, they are inadvertently reenacting it through the language they use to argue
their points. In other words, theologians are trying to out
talk the devil with Beelzebub as their speech coach.

Throughout this book, I argue that this flaw in contemporary accounts of social sin can be partially attributed to a
tendency of theologians to be insufficiently aware of the interaction between their own figures and metaphors and the
language of the culture in which they speak. Given that they

are quite concerned to describe and diagnose social evils, this blindness to the social evils embedded in their own linguistic patterns of thought and plays of language is rather surprising. This failure is not just unfortunate; it can have deleterious consequences. If theologians were to attend to such dimensions, they would be more aware of the social effects that their theological accounts might produce in their given social contexts—not just in terms of ideas but also in terms of social images. Attention to context should be a prerequisite for the construction of a doctrine of sin that seeks to effectively engage it in its social dimensions. If theologians carefully consider the language they use to develop and deploy descriptions of social sin, they will construct theological analyses that act as incisive tools for fighting against it rather than serving as its mirror.

Do No Harm is a rhetorical analysis of several influential doctrines of sin that looks specifically at the multiple ways these doctrines employ destructively stereotypic language and images in their accounts of sin in its social dimension. Chapter 1 in particular shows that when theologians fail to take into account the rhetorical context in which their doctrines are being deployed, they can inadvertently construct accounts of sin that depend on and play off of popular but nonetheless deeply problematic and oppressive discursive economies. The theologian's doctrine of sin is then caught in the strange position of rhetorically reproducing the very sin it is critiquing. If theologians want to achieve congruence between the content and the form of a discourse about social sin, it is vitally important for them to remain aware of the rhetorical arena in which they make their statements. In chapter 2 I look at the work of Reinhold Niebuhr, whom I have chosen because he offers an excellent example of what

I will call the abandonment of responsibility model of social sin-talk. In chapter 3 I turn to the work of Dietrich Bonhoeffer because his work on social sin is a cogent example of the model of sin essentialized as defilement. Chapter 4 examines the dominant stream of influence in the Protestant tradition about sin: the thought of Augustine of Hippo. A significant piece of this retrieval of the Augustinian take on sin will focus on two seminal Reformation thinkers whose works clearly influenced both Niebuhr and Bonhoeffer, and who continue to influence numerous contemporary Protestant theologians who write on sin: Martin Luther and John Calvin. The Protestant appropriation of the Augustinian tradition's view of sin provides insights that militate against some of the problematic discourse of Niebuhr and Bonhoeffer. This model of sin-talk is one that present-day theologians might productively engage.

Do No Harm is as a resource for helping theologians assume a kind of Hippocratic oath. Although theologians do not routinely take a vow of practice, as do doctors, most Christian theologians understand their work to maintain the health and well-being of the community of faith. In this regard, we, as theologians, are a type of practitioner. The healing art that we practice is the revelation of the restorative and transformative power of the Christian faith. When our sin-talk results in avoidable harm to persons and communities, it is more a case of unintended consequence than deliberate malice. The goal of this book is to help theologians engaged in sin-talk be better practitioners by offering tools that help us anticipate the consequences of our work.

1

THE SINS OF SIN-TALK

The Character of Sin-Talk

Let me illuminate my claim about the peculiar relation between our language about social sin and our social context by first looking at the unique character of sin-talk. As anyone familiar with the long Christian tradition of speaking about sin is aware, sin-talk is a challenging business. While theologians often have no problem defining sin in the abstract, when actually describing sin in concrete terms they find its subject matter more elusive. Once defined, sin seems neither univocal in nature nor transparent in character. When the term is applied to lived experience, there always seems to be a nagging voice saying, "Hold on a minute! Is it really that cut-and-dried?" It is precisely this cautionary voice that reminds us that while as Christians we must engage in sin-talk (it's part of the faith we claim), it is a precarious enterprise—it frequently misses the mark. We are prone to get it wrong. Our experiences resist it. Further, theologians have long been aware that getting it wrong can be a serious matter. Why? Because of two claims deeply embedded in the Christian worldview—sin destroys, and God punishes sin. Sin-talk is therefore serious business because once the source of social sin is named, the impulse to stigmatize it is strong and the desire to destroy it even stronger. In this regard, how we define sin in concrete terms strongly determines the character of our social actions against it.

As history has amply shown, the impulse to act against sin harbors deeply destructive potential. Douglas John Hall captures this dimension of sin-talk in his signaling of the potential dangers that attend Christian views of sin. "The vocabulary of Christian faith suffers from misunderstanding at every turn, but no term is as badly understood in both society and church as the little word, 'sin.' Nor is this misconception an innocent or merely 'religious' affair. Lives are ruined by it. Sometimes it destroys whole communities."[1] As I argue in the pages ahead, the harms that follow from social sin-talk that misses the mark are multiple. At the most obvious level, when theologians who seek to diagnose and address social sin misconstrue the social dynamics at work in a given situation, they risk inadvertently obscuring more decisive social forces at work. In other words, when their depiction of social sin fails to include an accurate account of the social forces producing it, the more important social and material relations that are fundamentally unjust are left unchallenged. When this happens, social sin-talk becomes the proverbial opium of the people—it covers up exactly what needs to be contested.

We may detect another trend among the harms of sin-talk described by Hall. In the history of the doctrine of sin, there is a consistent tendency for sin to be downwardly localized. For example, the cultural discourse about sin has increasingly focused–often subtly and imperceptibly–on the actions of persons and groups within society who have the least social power and are therefore especially vulnerable to social and economic injustice. This means that the "sinners" of our popular imagination have been those least able to contest the labeling of themselves and their social environment as sinful. Two examples of this are the current public discussions of welfare and sexual orientation–discussions in which people who receive welfare and gay people have frequently been silenced or discounted. Sin-talk regarding welfare, which focuses on irresponsibility, and sin-talk regarding sexual orientation, which focuses on disease, corruption, and defilement, are particularly interesting examples because they display the two forms of sin-talk described earlier. As I will illustrate further, these forms of sin-talk have slightly different social implications: The first creates a social margin that the second essentializes.

I pause here to make explicit a set of pairings that will be important throughout this book. The relationships of false attribution are (1) irresponsibility as a reason for the creation of social margins (irresponsibility/marginalization), and (2) defilement by the essentialization of the social margin (defilement/essentialization). These pairings theoretically represent the mechanics of how marginalizing discursive enactments become instantiated in material social reality. The first pairing indicates the way that the discourse of irresponsibility actually creates a liminal social space into which those who are deemed noncontributing

members of society may be corralled. The second pairing
points to the way that socially "miscreant" behaviors are
rendered such that they are interpreted as being part of the
very fabric of certain persons' being. In the paragraphs that
follow I will amplify the workings of these discursive practices and their social instantiations using two discrete examples, but here I want to notice the theoretical relationship
between these pairs.

The first pairing, irresponsibility/marginalization, that
theoretically supports the creation of a liminal social space
relies on the presumption that there exist two primary
groupings of persons within society: those whose presence
is necessary and who therefore contribute to the well-being
of society, and those whose presence is ambiguous and who
therefore are potentially harmful to social well-being.[2] Typically, those in the first group are persons who generally occupy places of social and economic privilege, while the
latter designation is reserved for those on the bottom rungs
of society's ladder. In the contemporary United States the
line drawn between these groups is the same as that drawn
between the "middle class" and the "underclass." More often
than not the fissure between the "necessary" and "not necessary" groups is mediated not in the language of class, but
rather in the discourse of social morality–values. So the
moral fabric of society is what is understood to be at issue
when this distinction is drawn. The implicit assumption at
work here is that the former group (the middle class), by the
very quality of its existence, strengthens society's moral life,
and the latter (the underclass) rends that fabric. In this particular instance of social marginalization, the despised group
is depicted as having within its power the capacity to produce responsible members of society, but not the quality of

dependability that will ensure that they "do the right thing"–hence, the ambiguity of its existence. Because the structure of the discourse concerns itself with inhabiting social space in a morally responsible way, the ambiguity of the marginalized group is rendered primarily as a moral issue. Accordingly, it becomes a moral duty of society to enforce maintenance of the liminal social space that these others occupy.

The second pairing, defilement/essentialization, relies on a powerful presumption as well. This presumption is that there are those persons and groups within society who by the very way that they exist, apart from any activities they may engage in, exemplify social and moral decay and disruption. Their presence is one that challenges the presumptive moral order of society, and hence is viewed as unnatural and dangerous. The technical term for this way of existing is *defilement*. The perceived disruption of the moral order caused by the defiling presence of an "unnecessary" group is of the gravest significance because, as Mary Douglas reminds us, it can result in a situation where "the blessing is withdrawn, and the power of the curse unleashed," leaving only "barrenness, pestilence, confusion."[3] The upshot of this presumption is that persons who, by their mode of existence, disrupt the moral universe are presented as a danger not only to themselves, but to the whole of society. Consequently, it becomes a significant moral responsibility of society to police, and in some instances destroy, those who defile the social order by disrupting the moral order with their presence.[4] This responsibility holds even when the persons or communities so identified are apparently contributing members of society. We see this phenomenon in situations like that of Jewish citizens under the Nazi regime or gay Christians in contemporary North

American Protestant church life. In both cases, demonization depends not on an observation of how people actually live their lives, but only on how their essential identity is rendered in public discourse. So for the set of relationships represented by the idea of defilement/essentialization, what we have is a depiction of persons who, because of the way their very being is discursively rendered, are deserving of extraction from the social body.

The relationship between these pairings is also significant. The first discursive practice–establishment of a social margin with the discourse of irresponsibility–draws the line that creates what I have termed the liminal social space, while the second discursive practice–the essentialization of marginalized groups as defiling–ensures that the occupants of this space will not routinely have the power to remove themselves from it. Each pairing is a discursive symbolization of the impulses within society toward the conservation of a particular set of social relations. They show the categorical ways of socially rendering groups as antithetical to normativity. Put another way, these are complementary moments in the construction of the social "other."

Sin-talk figures prominently in this discussion because while the overt subject matter is largely the structure of social relationships, the discursive practices underlying the destructive maintenance of this order are conceptually couched in the language of sin and morality. As a result, Christian theological discourse becomes implicated in the material harm caused to persons and communities by these discursive enactments. The very project of talking about social sin can, itself, become a profound instance of sin. To clarify the connection I am making, a review of specific instances of the sins of sin-talk might prove helpful: the "welfare queen" so ubiquitously rendered in recent debates on welfare reform, and "the homosexual" so prominent in contemporary Protestant rhetoric.[5]

Stone Her!
Sin-Talk and the Drama of the *Welfare Queen*

Let us look at how images of social sin play themselves out in debates over welfare reform. During much of the welfare reform debate in the 1980s and 1990s, headline accounts described the problem the nation faces as the abandonment of responsibility. According to this depiction of our nation's "sin," society has abandoned its responsibility to create self-sufficient citizens by establishing an artificial environment in which whole segments of the population are "taken care of." In this environment, we are told, those people who "are taken care of" lose their fear of hunger, homelessness, and disease along with their desire to work. They lose these basic fears—which normally drive people to work hard and participate in the social contract—because the government has made them dependent. In their dependent state, they lose any sense of social responsibility. While this particular discourse could have used a number of images, it is instructive to note that the central image that has come to symbolize this pathologically dependent person is the *welfare queen*—a sexually irresponsible, young, urban (code word for non-white) woman on welfare.

This image is vividly displayed in the writings of the sometimes political scientist, sometimes ethicist Lawrence Mead. In his essay "The Poverty Debate and Human Nature,"[6] he identifies this caricature as both the face and the cause of poverty:

Poverty is not new. Western societies have always contained destitute people, and there has always been debate over how to cope with them. But poverty was largely a local concern. In America it became prominent as a national issue in the 1960s. Three changes largely explain this. One is that the poor are much more obtrusive to the better-off today than a generation ago. Many rural people, particularly blacks from the South and Hispanics from Mexico and Puerto Rico, have moved to Northern cities, where they are more visible. . . . A second change is that today's poor are notably less self-reliant than yesteryear's. Serious poverty usually arises, at least in the first instance, from the lifestyle of the poor themselves. Most often, the initial cause is that poor parents have children out of wedlock, the fathers do not support them, and the mothers go on welfare rather than work themselves.[7]

Note that disguised in the figure that Mead conjures are images that cast her in the role of sinner. First, there is the image of the sexually irresponsible woman, which brings along with it the image of unsacramentalized sexual activity ("children out of wedlock"). Second, there is the image of aberrant matriarchy. According to Mead, these young women preside over weak families who are prone to misanthropic social behaviors, that is, families who produce offspring better termed *urban predators* than children.[8] These predatory scions respect neither property nor person and pose a mortal threat to order within our entire society.[9] This situation is clearly evil and, in the Christian logic of things, rooted in sin—particularly for a society imbued with the Protestant work ethic and respect for property.

And so the argument goes. The irresponsibility of the welfare queen is taken as a given; the job of society, in this account, is to figure out how to make her "responsible." Within this depiction of a social reality, we clearly see the discursive construction of a social margin. In order to begin evaluating this depiction, we must ask whether the *welfare queen*, upon whom this argument turns, refers to anyone or anything that exists unambiguously in reality. Or, is it rather manifestly a figure whose reality is linked to the margin which it by definition transgresses? I am not arguing, of course, that there are not mothers who receive public assistance of some sort. I am highlighting the way a liminal social space is constructed and persons are essentialized into it: The very terms that become the referent to this figure create a situation in which the only discourse possible is one that is a purely negative psychosocial analysis. The acceptance of the truth of the *welfare queen* entails an acceptance of the presupposed irresponsibility of this figure. This identity is one that takes primacy over all others (at least concerning the larger society), and thus functions as an essential identity. It is read as essential because it presumes that the *welfare queen*'s social position bespeaks something fundamental about her being and place within the social order. Let me clearly state that this phenomenon is not simply playing with words; this discursive practice has very real material consequences.

The discursive reality and subsequent social margin created around the figure of the *welfare queen* is a destructively simplistic one that does not take seriously the factors that influence her social space, such as the disintegrating effects of urban de-industrialization or of the housing exclusion that resulted from the suburbanization of the emerging service industry during the 1970s and 1980s; nor does it recognize the demise of quality education in urban America during the technological revolution, which located virtually all living-wage employment in skilled vocations.[10] Consequently, the conditions of grinding poverty that many in our nation endure are spuriously attributed exclusively to the pathological communities of the *welfare queen* and her scions. The problem is thus framed in terms of dealing with the irresponsibility of the *welfare queen* and not in terms of the need for society to interpret what equality and opportunity mean in a postindustrial age.

It is important to note the implicit–and less than obvious–discourse of sin. That is to say, the conceptual form and currency of the welfare reform discussion are directly related to a Christian discourse of sin and morality. So, while words like *responsibility* and *values* are used, sin is nevertheless implied in a subterranean manner. This subtext of sin moves closer to the surface when commentators such as Mead make an unmediated connection between sociopolitical expectation and religious responsibility:

> The New Testament call for liberation, however, does not occur in a vacuum. It is not directed against public expectation as such. The gospel takes for granted the entire structure of norms that Israel inherited from the Old Testament. Jesus says that he came to fulfill the law, not to overthrow it (Matt. 5:7-19). He teaches that people should relate to each other, and to God, out of love rather than legalism. But law is still necessary in a fallen society. St. Paul did not hesitate to "command" church members "living in idleness" to earn their own living (2 Thess. 3:10-12). For a Christian the law does not "save"

spiritually, but it remains a valid statement of God's will.
. . . We are a law- and lawyer-ridden society, but law in
the moral sense of a public code of behavior has sadly
declined. That itself is one cause of the social problem.
Today's Americans, and especially the poor, need to accept the law as "right" and as "fine gold" (Ps. 19:8, 10).[11]

This type of unexamined imputation of sin to a particular group flattens the nebula of circumstances in which the
group supposedly propagates its sin. It precludes a theological response critiquing both the construction of such figures as the *welfare queen* and subsequent public policy that
responds to these figures (1) because it passes off the *welfare
queen* as having a univocal referent in reality, and (2) because
it represents the "sins" of her (supposedly homogenous)
group one-dimensionally. In essence, concerned theologians are asked to debate within a discourse of stereotypes
and decontextualized behaviors, which, taken at face value,
seem indefensible because they are depicted as a deliberate
affront to our social and moral value system.

The consistently reinforced ignorance of how social,
political, and economic conditions influence this social sin
invites the conclusion that the only culpable parties are the
welfare queen and those who provide the services that allow
her to be pathologically dependent (i.e., the Pension and
Welfare Benefits Administration of the U.S. Department of
Labor).[12] This sort of analysis, which does not acknowledge
the social forces that create both the stereotype and the situation that the actual woman exists in, is wrongheaded and
dangerous: It distracts the larger society from the reality of
enforced localization of poverty and long-term, systemic
economic exclusion and social marginalization that are

antithetical to the health of a democratic culture. Sin-talk thus migrates from being an important reflection on the character, and finally the justness, of concrete relationships within society, to being a theological rationale for social marginalization and exclusion. While these may seem shop worn terms in our contemporary context, we cannot forget that sociopolitical marginalization and economic exclusion can mean the difference between health and hunger, college and prison, life and death.

Deadly Consequences: Sin-Talk, Sexual Orientation, and AIDS

Having used the example of the mythic *welfare queen* to illumine one popular model of social sin-talk–the responsibility model–and its creation of a sociopolitical margin, let us now turn to our second example, homophobic accounts of homosexuality, to explore the model of sin as defilement/essentialization. While there are many similarities between the ways in which the *welfare queen* and *the homosexual* are constructed in our contemporary culture, the topic of sexual orientation differs from welfare in that many homophobic accounts of *homosexuals* depict them not only as abandoning social responsibility, but as defiling and corrupting the natural order of things.[13] While these images of pollution are not completely missing in the responsibility model, in the case of homosexuality, the rhetoric of defiling nature comes to the fore with exacting force. The example of sexual orientation also differs from welfare in the degree to which explicitly theological reasoning is used to support depictions of defilement and pollution. As I have argued, when the *welfare queen* is mythically rendered, the appropriation of theological grounds for that rendering are usually implicit and diluted with secular terms. In the case of negative accounts of *homosexuals*, however, the appropriation of theological grounds for that construction is not only obvious, it is foundational.

Anyone familiar with the debates in Protestant church bodies in North America knows that present-day communities of faith are deeply conflicted about the issue of sexual orientation. Until recent years, the preponderance of Christian reflection on human sexuality has lifted up heterosexuality as the normative model of human sexual relations and has subsequently labeled same-gender relationships and sexual activity as sin. The rationale for this negative account of homosexuality has, in Protestant circles, been drawn from Scripture and from related doctrinal accounts of what the ideal marriage between man and woman should be. While scriptural and doctrinal evidence on this matter is certainly not unambiguous, the sensibility of the mainstream Christian tradition has been, until recently, nearly univocal: Same-gender sexual relations are an abomination; they are unequivocally wrong. This position is concisely summarized in the following statement, which represents the attitudes in many Protestant churches across the country today. "Jesus asked, 'Wilt thou be made whole?' To such a question, which the Saviour still asks today, the homosexual sincerely desiring help must admit the sin of his past life, repent, accept forgiveness, and begin the struggle against his old nature."[14] In statements such as this, one finds ample evidence of what I have described as a defilement/essentialization model of sin-talk. In this context, *homosexuals* are depicted not only as doing bad things, but also as inherently corrupt in their being, in their "old nature."

Far from being simply good people acting irresponsibly, they are "polluting the natural order." Not just their acts but their existence is considered repulsive. In many cases, this depiction suggests that because they offend the natural order of human relations, they are somehow less than human.

Notice that the lines of the discourse follow closely the model of defilement suggested by Paul Ricoeur in *The Symbolism of Evil*, in which he uses the theoretical framework within which the idea of defilement has meaning.[15] According to Ricoeur, this framework is built on ontological reality. The uncleanness that characterizes the defiling agent is writ such that it becomes a part of the definition of the agent's existence: The problem is not what *the homosexual* does, but that *the homosexual* exists at all.

The damaging effects of this view of same-sex relationships have been and continue to be profound. Both in individual lives and at a broader social level, this form of stigmatization has led to acts of violence and exclusion, only a few of which are now reaching the public consciousness of North Americans. One example of the social harms produced by the exclusionary logic of this form of sin-talk is the modern day reality of HIV/AIDS. Throughout much of the gestation period of this plague, the entire issue was treated by society and by much of the church as a purely moral issue—because of its association with an "immoral lifestyle"—and not as a medical issue. The results of this attitude toward the disease have been devastating. During the early stages of the epidemic when proactive research and educational intervention could have made the most significant impact, resources were made scarce. Because it was a disease associated with sinful people, it was not as aggressively treated as it should have been.

This demonstrates well the degree to which theological depictions of sin can lead to deeply problematic social practices. In this instance we see clearly how the supposed culpability of the afflicted plays a decisive role in forming the character of society's–and the church's–unhelpful responses to their suffering. By condoning the oppression of gay persons, both before and during the nascent stages of the epidemic, many churches became complicit in the plague that is sweeping throughout much of the underdeveloped world. Ironically, even now, when many churches–even very conservative ones–are engaged in various sorts of AIDS ministries, they continue to carry partial responsibility for the ravaging that is taking place in communities around the world.

Resisting Dangerous Assumptions

Having considered how the discursive rendering of the *welfare queen* and *the homosexual* illustrates some of the perils of sin-talk, let us now explore some current theological trends that resist the dangerous logic discussed above. Here I will rely solely on a theological approach to sexual orientation to make my point (although the approach is equally applicable to the welfare issue).

As recent research in the history of sexual orientation and theology has made clear, there are a number of complicated ways in which the church and its theology have participated in the marginalization and stigmatization of homosexuality and hence in the spread of AIDS. I want to lift up one particular feature of the church's reasoning about homosexuality as a sin: the church's inability to adopt what has been called a "consequentialist" attitude toward its assessment of this form of "social sin." By the term *consequentialist*, I mean to identify a posture that takes seriously the concrete results of the church's practices and proclamations for persons and communities. A consequentialist attitude takes seriously, for example, these questions offered by Christopher Morse in his book *Not Every Spirit: A Christian Dogmatics of Disbelief*: "Does the spirit [of the practice or proclamation] increase love? Does it produce what the prophets called true peace, or *shalom*? Does it further God's righteous justice? Does it provide liberation? Does it up build the community (not to be confused with mere earthly success)?"[16] In essence, what Morse is pointing to, and what a consequentialist approach does, is recognizing that a criterion for theological discourse must explicitly be disseminating God's *shalom* in the world. To better understand a consequentialist approach to discussing social sin, let us look at the dynamics of theological reflection at work in some of the churches that have rejected the traditional position that homosexuality is a sin, and have taken much more positive views of same-sex relationships.

In recent years, many communions within the church have begun to reassess their tradition's evaluation of homosexuality. While this reassessment has involved careful study of Scripture and critical engagement with traditional positions, one of the most important elements in this discernment process has been the willingness of these communities to listen to the stories of people involved in same-sex relationships. In this context, the testimonies of gay and lesbian men and women about their sexual identities and relationships has been an important source of understanding for this particular form of human relationality. In contrast to communities who have rendered gays and lesbians voiceless, in these communities the actual voices of gay persons are taken seriously. Their testimonies have made it clear to anyone who takes people who are speaking in good faith at their word that the relationships in which these persons are involved are not capricious and willfully perverted "lifestyle choices"; rather, they are loving and faithful actualizations of their humanity before God.

This move to listen to the voices of the "sinful" has proved crucial in the church's assessment of its doctrine of sin. In recent years, virtually every instance of the church's "changing its mind" about a particular social or economic view of sin has involved actually listening to the testimony of those considered sinful. For example, the role of the slave narrative in the church's reevaluation of the institution of chattel slavery is undeniable. Similarly, the testimony of women who are theologians and laypersons has occasioned a reassessment of doctrine and has led to changes in, among other things, the status of women in the ordained ministry. In both these instances, one sees how considering the testimony of persons and communities who have hitherto been labeled "sinners" can lead to enormous shifts in perception and policy. The voices of marginalized people have been harbingers of transformation within the church's understanding of itself and the world.

I offer this account of the role that this testimony has played in contemporary reassessments of sin as one example of a mechanism by which the church is enabled to see its own sins. Yet there are many other ways, several of which I will explore in the chapters ahead. It suffices now to say that the testimony of persons who are being marginalized by theological discourse is a fundamental component in a consequentialist approach to social sin.

I believe that in these shifts we are witnessing the evolution of the Christian community's understanding of human existence and the nature of sin. They are occurring because the church has been willing to reassess its assumptions about the sinners it has posited, and it is doing so by listening to their voices. At the heart of these shifts is a change in perception about what makes someone a sinner. I use the term *sinner* here in a particular way. What I refer to as "sinners" are those people whom the church has chosen to depict not as basically good people who do bad things, but persons who have been identified as "sinful" in their very person, above and beyond any particular action or any general implication in the sin that characterizes the human condition. As we see in the figure of the stigmatized *homosexual*, the sinner is the one considered *essentially* corrupted and defiled. What we see happening in churches that are reassessing their understanding of sexual orientation is that when the testimony of this kind of "sinner" is heard, the church is able to recognize the degree to which false biases have formed the logic of its view of such persons. In a word, these communions have begun to deal constructively with the presence of gay and lesbian persons by accepting them as real persons whose sexual identity is but one aspect of their personhood and not definitive of it.

This positive evolution in the church's understanding of what human beings are and how we think about sin is rooted in the fact that the Christian tradition has a demand for consequentialist introspection deep within its logic. This is to say that in its true form the Christian tradition is concerned about the social consequences of its pronouncements and practices upon the lives of persons and communities. When it is true to itself, Christian theology asserts that if par-

ticular construals of a doctrine or a scriptural interpretation
are found to have the sustained consequence of harming
certain persons and communities, these construals and in-
terpretations need to be called into question. Frequently, this
calling into question leads to the realization by the church
that aspects of its current modes of scriptural interpretation,
ecclesial practice, and public pronouncement do not live up
to the overarching standard of faithful living that the Christian community holds for itself. Peter Damian describes this
process well in *The Book of Gomorrah*. He writes:

> These exercises in biblical and historical scholarship are
> not luxuries which heirs of the Christian tradition may
> or may not undertake. Christianity is a religion rooted in
> the Bible and tradition, not simply in the sense that it
> has a past but in the sense that it draws its food and
> nourishment through these roots. . . . It is only through
> such studies that the heirs of the Christian tradition will
> be able to move beyond their history, with self-con-
> scious understanding of the past and a reasoned rejec-
> tion of some facets of the tradition, toward a new
> synthesis in response to the demands and insights of
> today.[17]

The process that Damian describes is one that has gone on
in each generation since the apostles in Jerusalem made
peace with Paul's mission to the Gentiles, and it continues
today in churches where a critical reassessment of homosexuality is occurring.

    In contrast, what one finds in churches that continue to
posit *the homosexual* as sinner is, among other things, a collective refusal to incorporate consequentialist reasoning

into the community's process of theological reflection. Because they refuse to consider the effects that their position has upon personal lives and communal actions, they do not afford themselves a lively existential starting point for critically reflecting on the biases hidden in their accounts. If they would pause to listen to the voices of those they stigmatize, they might realize that their judgments about these persons' status as sinners are rooted in the church's uncritical acceptance of cultural conventions that are homophobic and heterosexist rather than in purely reasoned reflection on Scripture and the tradition. Instead of adopting a consequentialist openness that would allow them to reconsider their position, they settle for an ossified understanding of "immorality" that refuses to acknowledge the problematic cultural conventions that undergird it.

As I hope the examples of the mythic *welfare queen* and *the homosexual* make clear, sin-talk is a complicated matter that needs to be treated with great care. In the pages ahead, I will describe how one way for theologians to treat sin-talk with care is to be ever vigilant about how oppressive patterns of thought can creep into our discourse about sin. These patterns may be rooted in displacement of persons to liminal social spaces by particular sociopolitical discourses, as in the case of welfare, and they may also be rooted in theological assumptions about the nature of true personhood and the margins these assumptions create, as in the case of homosexuality. Susan Davies describes these two dynamics with compelling clarity:

> The oppression of any group, such as women; people of color; gay men and lesbians; the poor; the physically, mentally, or emotionally disabled; or the old, begins

with a defined norm of personhood. Such a norm is a standard, sometimes unspoken, that declares who is most real, the most fully human, the most acceptable kind of person in any given situation. Oppression has its origins in the use of that standard to judge all people and to enforce the exclusion or punishment of those who do not meet the standard. Those outside the standards are experienced as "other" by those who fit the norm, and treated as though they were less than fully human.[18]

What we have, then, is the primary concern of a consequentialist approach to sin-talk: It does not participate in the marginalization of any of God's children.

Mind Pictures: Paying Attention to Discursive Realities

Having looked briefly at two examples of social sin-talk in present-day culture, let me now say a few words about my earlier statement that many contemporary Protestant theologians fail to develop adequate doctrines of social sin because they do not take into consideration the social worlds within which their theologies are formulated and deployed. The problem of Christian sin-talk's participation in social and economic oppression is not limited to headline discussions of welfare or church debates over the status of same-sex relationships. While there are many reasons for this situation, I believe that a primary cause is that too often Christian sin-talk is insulated from a thoroughgoing analysis of what I refer to loosely as a theologian's "linguistic social context."

The phrase *linguistic social context* refers to the highly complex wealth of images, linguistic conventions, language patterns, and figures that constitute the pool of terms we use to name and make sense of our world. In the language of contemporary theory, these patterned but often chaotic images are described as "discursive economies," which are those mixtures of language, images, and even practices that provide the reference points we use to interpret reality. They are the complex of ideas and customs of knowing that underlie particular forms of our cultural and social "common sense." Discursive economies reflect and legitimate specific relations of power and social hierarchy in a given context, as well as provide a conceptual space in which these relations can be enacted.[19]

To demonstrate what I mean by discursive economy, let us look at a particular cultural image that has become popular in recent North American public discourse—the image of the "soccer mom." In the cultural imagination of American society, this figure has become popular because of the associations it conjures up, many of which remain unnamed. Most people who find the term useful would probably tell you that it refers, quite simply, to mothers who are harried by the extracurricular activities of their children. Closer inspection of the images associated with this busy mom, however, make it clear that when evoked, she is not just a neutral image. Encoded in the term *soccer mom* is a variety of additional associations. To use the language of theory, the image is dependent upon a number of discursive economies—it represents the intersection of several cultural discourses. Specifically, the figure reflects late-twentieth-century North American cultural discourses related to gender (motherhood), sexuality (heterosexuality), socioeconomic stratification (suburban, middle-class), race (*soccer moms* are rarely pictured as nonwhite), and ethnicity ("generic" Northern European). The seemingly simple image of the *soccer mom* is in actuality a multilayered complex of cultural assumptions and sensibilities. In her exemplification of these cultural discourses the figure of the *soccer mom* serves as a discursive antitype for the *welfare queen* and the *"feminist" lesbian* and an alternate type for the *career mom*. It is undeniable that in this role the *soccer mom* figure has played prominently in social policy formation and political campaigns of the last decade. This is precisely the character of discursive economies: No matter how simple they seem, their use implicates cultural discourses that may be subtextual but are nonetheless powerful, and highly political.

It is my contention that too often theologians are not cognizant of the ways they use and are used by the discursive economies that they employ in their sin-talk. This is evident in the two examples I considered. In the first instance (welfare reform), the discursive economy surrounding the *welfare queen* ("breeding" irresponsibility and lawlessness) was seen to be used in a damaging fashion to frame a social policy debate that conceptually demonizes a largely powerless segment of our society. This is a discursive economy that, while ostensibly commenting on social and economic issues, is actually using subtextual images and language to discuss sin and morality. In this regard, the public policy debate has been framed by the logic of a morality play. To the extent that theologians have intervened in this debate using the figure of the *welfare queen*, they have been complicit in the enactment of punitive social policies against one of the least powerful segments of our society.

The second case (homosexuality) is an instance of the language of sin working to reify aspects of tradition in unhelpful and destructive ways. Here we were reminded of the

necessity to be concerned about the consequences attend-
ing the intervention of sin–talk in ecclesial and cultural con-
troversies. The lack of a consequentialist approach to
interpreting the tradition was demonstrated to negatively
affect the character of Christian engagements with sin in its
social dimension.

These are but two examples of the propensity of sin–
talk to go awry in cultural and ecclesial interventions. They
are instances of what Serene Jones calls "the sin of sin–talk,"
that is, cases of sin–talk used as a discourse of destruction.[20]
These examples of what I call "misconceiving sin" are helpful in identifying the importance of paying attention to how
sin is handled discursively. In each case the notion of sin is
circumscribed in such a manner that a fitting response
would likely be destructive of both persons and communities. In essence, these discursive renderings create an inver-
sion of the putative Christian logic of sin. Instead of sin
being the destroyer and the faithful response the remedy,
the "appropriate" response wreaks at least as much havoc as
the underlying sin is purported to have created.

How might theologians avoid the reification of culturally problematic images in their doctrines of sin? While it is
certainly impossible for any thinker to completely extricate
herself from the discursive logic of the culture in which she
finds herself, she can take steps that make her work more
self–critical with respect to the language she uses. To pro-
mote this self–critical posture, I have found it useful to ask
two sets of questions when I approach not only the writings
of other theologians, but also my own constructive work as
a theologian. First, I ask: What are the seemingly common-
sense images that are being used in this construction? What
types of figures are being deployed? What seemingly in-

nocuous depictions of persons are at work? Having identified these figures, I then ask a second, even more important set of questions: What kind of social power relations undergird these images? What do these cultural images mean in their context with respect to social relations? This means asking further: Are they oppressively gendered, racist, classist, homophobic, heterosexist, or anti-Semitic? It involves asking, in short, Are oppressive social dynamics being played out in these images? In the next three chapters, I ask these questions as I approach the work of five theologians who have been enormously influential in contemporary Protestant thought about social sin: Reinhold Niebuhr, Dietrich Bonhoeffer, Augustine of Hippo, Martin Luther, and John Calvin.

Definitely Not the Way It's Supposed to Be!

Before turning to the work of these theologians, a brief look at a more contemporary work on the doctrine of sin will lend itself to the kind of critical analysis I will do of Niebuhr and Bonhoeffer. It is the recent work of Cornelius Plantinga, *Not the Way It's Supposed to Be: A Breviary of Sin.*[21] I deal with this work in order to demonstrate that the issues I raise with Niebuhr and Bonhoeffer are not simply antiquarian oddities, but rather very real issues that theologians writing about sin face today.

I chose Plantinga's work for two reasons. First, his work is explicitly concerned with sin in its social dimension: Plantinga is concerned about sin as an issue not only in the personal life of the human person, but in the effects that it has on the common life of humanity. Second, this book takes seriously the categories that emerge from traditional

Christian grapplings with the issue of sin. Plantinga's work is one I sympathize with, for it is not my purpose to challenge Protestant sin-talk that engages social sin per se, but rather to identify problematic tendencies that diminish the very real value of the project. My critique of Plantinga's work should not, therefore, be read as a blanket indictment of the project of recovering traditional theological categories to interpret social sin. Rather, it should be seen as an objection to an instance when this recovery is done in a way that is destructive to the dignity and well-being of marginalized persons and communities. My reasons for this assessment of Plantinga's work will become apparent in the following critique of the assumptions at work in his book.

Not the Way It's Supposed to Be can be placed within a trajectory of contemporary sin-talk that I identified as the responsibility model. This stream within the literature of sin constructs sin-talk as a sociocultural category that is a necessary part of a healthy society. As the thinking goes, in the absence of some proper, shared sense of sin, a distorted picture of evil (and culpability for it) becomes the common currency. This distortion reduces a society's ability to distinguish between right and wrong, which greatly facilitates its degeneration. Notable among the works in this genre is Karl Menninger's *Whatever Became of Sin?*[22]

Although writing twenty years apart, Menninger and Plantinga offer a decidedly similar diagnosis for what ails American society. Each argues that the eclipse of a vibrant notion of sin has led to the demise of the concept of personal responsibility.[23] The effect of this absence has been the emergence of a general state of social irresponsibility, the fruits of which are seen in the fractured relations between persons and groups, and the propensity of society to be mesmerized in the face of evil. While neither Menninger nor Plantinga argues that a heightened sense of rectitude among the populace will magically repair the brokenness of society, each insists that a recovery of both the language of sin and the substantial intent of that language is an immediate and absolute necessity. This language is the rhetoric of responsibility.

The framework constructed by this rhetorical model specifically locates culpability for sin within particular enactments of agency, meaning that sin is the result of persons behaving poorly and irresponsibly. A goal of this method is therefore to lobby for an approach to sin-talk that not only recognizes the social results of sin but focuses attention on the behavior of culpable agents. It is with the sensibility expressed by this rhetoric that Plantinga pursues his work.

Plantinga begins his project with an articulation of the brokenness of our common life. In the schema he offers, this brokenness is both the occasion and the fruit of sin. The language that he uses to talk about this is the "breaking of shalom." By using this language, Plantinga wants to point simultaneously to the violation of some creaturely prerogative and to the disruption of the divine ordering of reality. Put another way, he amplifies the notion of the acts and inclinations that lead us to recite, "and forgive us our trespasses."

The scenario that Plantinga employs to make this brokenness evident is one in which an individual's plight ought to elicit compassion but instead calls forth a predatory response. He uses the opening scene from the movie *Grand Canyon* (1991) in which a hardworking lawyer faces the misfortune of having his car break down on a dark city street. As Plantinga recounts the scene, the man's

expensive car stalls on one of those alarming streets
whose teenage guardians favor expensive guns and
sneakers. The attorney does manage to phone for a tow
truck, but before it arrives, five young street toughs sur-
round his disabled car and threaten him with considerable harm. Then, just in time, the tow truck shows up. . . .
The toughs protest: the truck driver is interrupting their
meal.[24]

Immediately, two points become apparent in Plantinga's retelling of this scene. First, his choice to use this
movie scene suggests that he believes it renders some truth
about contemporary human reality. Viewed in this light it
becomes a metaphor for the predatory character of the bro-
ken human condition–helplessness is met with naked
avarice. Second, he seems to think that these characters
have some univocal referent in reality that makes drawing a
flat one-to-one correspondence between fiction and fact acceptable. These observations make it clear that in his re-
counting of this scene, Plantinga considers himself to be
truth-telling and not simply retelling a story.

This means that an analysis of Plantinga's work must
begin with an interrogation of the implicit claim that this
scene is in some important way truth-telling. Specifically,
we must ask, Are the constituent elements of the metaphor
truthful? If so, in what way do they express truth? If this
scene is not truthful, then we must ask, What does this particular scene, and Plantinga's use of it, express?

I contend that the elements of this metaphor do not
have the capacity to unequivocally express the truth Plantinga wishes them to–namely, typifying predatory brokenness. Rather, I suggest that their deployment as metaphor

says far more about his perception of reality than about reality itself. I make this claim because of a particularly glaring oversight in Plantinga's exercise of truth-telling through this scene. The oversight has to do with another moment of this opening sequence. Plantinga fails to recount the initial encounter between the "immigration lawyer" and the "street toughs." the toughs swagger up to the lawyer's car and ask in a seemingly mocking fashion, "So what, you need some help?" to which he replies, with immediately apparent fear, "Please, you can take my money, or the car, but don't hurt me." After this the interaction becomes more menacing and, as Plantinga does note, they threaten him with considerable bodily harm. This would be another oft-told tale of danger and violence on the mean streets of the urban jungle, and a perfect metaphor for speaking about the sinful brokenness within our society, were it not for one problem. The problem, which is better stated as a question, is, "Who sinned first?" On Plantinga's reading it seems clear, but is it really?

The initial exchange between the white man and the black teenagers (to put code words aside) is shot through with ambiguity. While it is true that the teenagers swagger as they approach the man, a posture that Plantinga finds menacing, it is also true that most young males affect some sort of swagger. While it is true that they ask if he needs help in a mocking fashion, it is also true that in many places this is the way people speak to strangers. The point I wish to make is that until the man opens his mouth, it is not self-evident that the intent of the young men is to rob or bring bodily harm to him. It is only clear what the intentions of the young men are if one assumes that they fit a particularly noxious cultural figure of young black males as malevolent *urban predators*. Certainly, this appears to be the lens through which the man in the movie, and Plantinga for that matter, sees what is going on.

The white man's response to the black teenagers brings an immediate shift in the character of the exchange. When the young men initially approached him and asked if he needed help, they were smiling, albeit in a derisive way. An immediate change occurs in their faces after the man says to them, "Please, you can take my money, or the car, but don't hurt me." The smiles fade. The boys become menacing. Is it that they have been unmasked? Or is it that they are insulted by being accused of being criminals by someone who knows nothing about them? Are they "criminals" when they approach him, or are they (like many teenagers) prone to live up to the expectation given in that moment? We simply don't know. What we do know is that the response of the man is totally unambiguous. He encounters a group of black teenagers on a city street at night and immediately assumes that they are thieves or worse. Does he see their "faces," or does he simply see the thugs that his culture conditions him to see?

Let me correlate this with another story. A few years ago at a meeting of one of the state boards of my denomination, the United Church of Christ, a woman shared with the group an extraordinary experience. A few nights before, she had been traveling south on I-91 in Connecticut and had run over something in the road that gave her a flat tire. This happened on a stretch of the road with no shoulder. She drove until she came to an exit and got off the highway. It wasn't until she reached the end of the ramp that she realized that she was in Bridgeport. This was in 1988–a time when Bridgeport, Connecticut, was commonly known as "little Beirut." She got off the ramp and pulled to the curb. Within minutes a car pulled up behind her. The music from the car was so loud that she could feel it. From the car emerged four dark figures. They swaggered up to her car and banged on the window. One of them asked her in a surly manner, "You need help, lady?" Terrified, but not knowing what to do, she said a quick prayer and answered "yes." The four boys spent the next half hour changing her tire. When they finished, they told her that this was a rough neighborhood and she had better get back on the highway. Would the story have ended differently if instead of asking for help, she had responded in the way that the man did in *Grand Canyon*? We simply don't know.

From a superficial perspective, the preceding situation was, as was the one in *Grand Canyon*, riddled with ambiguity. The outcome of neither situation was necessitated by the context or the persons involved. There may have been as much potential for good as for evil in each situation. In my estimation, a theologian should see this—particularly a theologian concerned with the issue of sin. The ambiguity of the situation in the movie seemingly escapes Plantinga. Yet recognition of the ambiguity that suffuses the situation depicted in the film renders two clear truths. First, the incapacity of this scene, as a cultural representation, to be a vehicle of truth-telling in an unambiguous way is exposed, which points to a second truth, namely, the way that assessments about sin, and sinners, are conditioned by cultural expectation. Cultural conditioning directly affects the way that the viewer sees sin and identifies sinners in a given circumstance. I believe Plantinga's failure to recognize the ambiguity of the scene and his attendant reading of the situation demonstrate both of these truths.

What we have, then, is a case of nearsightedness. In *Not the Way It's Supposed to Be*, Plantinga depends upon cultural images that, although readily accessible and pervasive, are unhelpful at best. His use of these images—the *urban predator* and the suburban victim—does not acknowledge their questionable truthfulness or, more troubling, their latent destructiveness. Can anyone deny that the recent hysteria about crime, and the attendant rise of the penal culture within our society, is intimately linked to fear of the *urban predator?* Who can forget the skillfully produced "Willie Horton ads" used in a not too distant past presidential campaign? Moreover, it seems that Plantinga is thoroughly uncritical of the problematic contribution to this hysteria made by *Not the Way It's Supposed to Be.* Specifically, its perpetuation of the notion of an inherent pathology symptomatic of the African American community as an explicit assumption, propagated in other works like Dinesh D'Souza's *The End of Racism: Principles for a Multiracial Society* and Richard Herrnstein and Charles Murray's *The Bell Curve: Intelligence and Class Structure in American Life.*[25] It thus seems that Plantinga is unaware of how his work participates in the cultural denigration and economic marginalization of persons and communities. The history of characterizing nonwhite communities and persons as corrupting influences within Western society is a long one, and this type of discursive marginalization has significant real-world consequences.

In Plantinga's work we find evidence of the problematic propensities of Christian sin–talk that I initially outlined. First, we see the tendency toward an inadequate appreciation for the context within which the theologian is writing. I have demonstrated how Plantinga uses the image of the *urban predator* without adequate notice of the way that contemporary American society both renders young nonwhite males (as wanton criminals) and responds to that rendering (i.e., a pervasive penal response). Second, I have identified how this first sort of oversight produces destructive consequences. The major deficiency in Plantinga's work is that it unwarily handles cultural stereotypes and images that destroy. The result is that even though the categories he uses are helpful for considering the workings of sin in its social dimension (i.e., violation of shalom), the content with which he infuses them is problematic. That is to say, using the concepts of corruption and brokenness as a framework within which to understand sin's workings in our contemporary context is a valuable undertaking, Plantinga just does it poorly. This is an obvious result of the failure to engage marginalized persons and communities about whom he is speaking beyond the caricatures that are created by biased cultural understandings and sensational headlines.[26] Moving beyond the biased discursive economies that are rife in our context might have helped Plantinga to see the ambiguity in the scene from *Grand Canyon* and perhaps led him to a different description of sin in that instance.

In essence, I contend that for a discourse of sin to be truly helpful, it must take into account more than titillating factoids and uninformed cultural "common sense." Otherwise, what ends up happening is what we find in *Not the Way It's Supposed to Be*–a useful retrieval of theological categories mitigated by unhelpful cultural sensibilities.

Summary

The purpose of this chapter has been to describe problems that arise in Christian enactments of sin-talk when theologians pay inadequate attention to their social and discursive contexts. I identified two sets of highly problematic tendencies in contemporary sin-talk that are constituent of this larger problem. To review, the two pairings are (1) the rhetorical construction of a social margin by way of the cultural discourse of irresponsibility, and (2) the essentialization of persons and communities into that margin by way of the identification of their being with defilement. To illustrate these tendencies, I outlined two general examples of sin-talk gone awry in the public square: welfare reform and the church's understanding of homosexuality. The welfare reform example illustrated the irresponsibility/marginalization model. Here we see a socially and economically marginalized group rhetorically constructed using Christian symbols and language subtextually in such a way that it is made the target of punitive social policy. In the instance of homosexuality, we see how the church's tradition is used to legitimate a discursive marginalization that identifies sin with the very being of a distinct group of persons and thereby conceptually–and deceptively–localizes sin in one segment of the population (the defilement/essentialization model). Following the identification of these two public enactments of destructive sin-talk, I analyzed the work of a theologian whose sin-talk illustrates the problems of structure and substance that can arise when inadequate attention is paid to the social implications of the language and images one deploys.

Our world and our society are rife with the material consequences of sin. Hunger, disease, war, oppression, and the destruction of the environment are all to real consequences experienced by many of God's children in their daily lives. Social sin is a reality that must be taken seriously and about which Christians must speak. We must remember, however, that for all the capacity that sin-talk has to help people of good will properly interpret sin in their social and cultural contexts, it has an antithetical capacity to brand with a scarlet letter those most despised by their society. In the following chapters I will amplify my description of problematic tendencies present in contemporary narrations of social sin. My scrutiny will focus on the works of Reinhold Niebuhr and Dietrich Bonhoeffer. I specifically focus on these thinkers because of their seminal influence on the work of social sin-talk during the twentieth century, and because they each write from a distinctly Protestant trajectory. This second point raises the question of whether the failures in their works point to some general weaknesses inherent to Protestant sin-talk. This question will be taken up further on in the book. For now, it suffices to recognize that our sin-talk has a problem—it frequently harms more than it helps. Now we will attempt to understand why this problem exists and begin the work of restoring the capacity of sin-talk to interpret the social sin that so tragically permeates our contemporary context.

2

CREATED BY GOD, CONSTRUCTED BY SIN

Niebuhr's Dilemma

Two facets of Reinhold Niebuhr's work—his theoretical explication of sin, which is found in such works as *The Nature and Destiny of Man*, and his public deployment of his notions of sin, which is found in his occasional pieces such as those appearing in *Christian Century*–illustrate the relationship between dominant discursive economies and sin-talk emerging from a Reformation trajectory. While Niebuhr provides an excellent description of the corruptions in power evident in modern Western society, his analysis fails to notice the discursive economies that undergird the systems that he critiques. By this I mean that Niebuhr does not give adequate attention to the ways the discourses that he both analyzes and deploys rhetorically construct marginalized persons and communities–the irresponsibility/marginalization model of sin-talk. As a consequence, he inadvertently develops a theological anthropology and a concomitant doctrine of sin that depend heavily on the objectification of marginalized persons and communities—the defilement/essentialization model of sin-talk. This dynamic is demonstrated most vividly in Niebuhr's discursive rendering of *the Negro*, as an objectified figure. In this instance, Niebuhr's accounts of both sin and marginalized persons move beyond describing their sins as endemic to them by virtue of their humanity, to creating an identity between sin and *Negro culture* such that the inhabitants of that culture can do nothing but sin. While Niebuhr sets out to describe some aspect of sin in its social dimension, what he actually accomplishes is the rhetorical creation of sinners.

I am not simply saying that if Niebuhr had adjusted his argumentation to take the marginalizing tendencies of the discourses he used into account that he might have avoided this problem and been more "politically correct." Self-examination of his rhetoric would have been helpful, but a significant problem may well have remained for Niebuhr: simply recognizing a particular negative usage of a stereotypic cultural figure does not automatically lead to the more penetrating insight that the very use of some cultural images predisposes sin-talk to participation in oppressive discursive and social economies. Nonetheless, Niebuhr is an important example of the dangers of unexamined deployment of dominant discursive economies.

The Contours of Niebuhr's Problem

Although there are a number of ways to analyze these troublesome aspects of Niebuhr's work, I will focus on the way that he conceives of the relationship between "primitive"

culture, individual agency, and sin. Specifically, I will analyze how his descriptive accounts of "primitive/backward"
cultures and the category "individuality" construct a rhetorical framework in which "primitive/backward" cultures are
denied the capacity to produce moral agents who, while yet
sinners, can transcend their immediate circumstance to pur-
sue justice through an enactment of their creaturely freedom. Given the importance that Niebuhr attributes to
creaturely freedom—"the essence of man is his freedom"—it
becomes apparent that by his description he is denying not
just the moral capacity of "primitive/backward" cultures,
but, to an extent, the humanity of the members of that culture.[1] At stake are the very terms upon which persons are
accepted and appreciated as being fully human. So the first
problematic formulation is Niebuhr's portrayal of "primitive" or "backward" cultures in his analysis of social sin suggests an equivalence between those cultures and the
primary unfortunate aspect of modern Western society—
unbridled social egoism that leads to the annihilation of the
individual.[2] By this Niebuhr is referring to contexts in which
the claims of the body politic are such that they impede the
actualization of individuality. I will take this up later in this
chapter, but it is important to note here that whereas
Niebuhr represents this as a failure of modern society in the
West, it is identified by him as a matter-of-fact aspect of
"primitive" or "backward" culture.[3] Thus we have Niebuhr's
contentions that "There is thus no spiritual basis in the Ori-
ent for what we know as the dignity of the individual" and
"Centuries may be required to change the sense of racial
kinship of African tribal primitivism to something similar to
the European sense of national kinship."[4] What we see in
these descriptions of primitive societies is that the proper

recognition of the individual, which is for Niebuhr the high-est aspiration for imperfect human societies, is completely absent from certain societies. Consequently, it seems that what Niebuhr finds to be the defining characteristic of sin-ful human society–the destruction of the individual–is sim-ply a given in primitive/backward cultures. Thus, Niebuhr implicitly sets up a hierarchy of sinful cultures.

The second problematic aspect of Niebuhr's doctrine of sin is his description of human agency or, more precisely, the facet of human agency that he identifies as being the nexus of sin–namely, the "undue claims by the self."[5] What I want to draw attention to in this chapter is a rhetorical di-mension of Niebuhr's account of this particular enactment of agency. I want to suggest that Niebuhr's scheme engages in a type of objectification of persons and communities that not only calls into question their status as moral agents but raises qualitative questions about their humanity. He does this by disallowing the type of agency necessary by his own account for persons to enact sin. As we shall see, when Niebuhr moves beyond abstract, conceptual accounts of sin and begins to describe concrete examples of sin in its social dimension, his rhetoric "embodies" sin in a way that, ironi-cally, constructs persons who by definition cannot sin.

The effect of these two marginalizing tendencies on Niebuhr's doctrine of sin is significant. Beyond being evi-dence of theological cultural imperialism, these problems demonstrate the difficulty of speaking about sin in its social dimension using the language and images of negative stereotypes. The rhetorical structure that Niebuhr's work in-habits is one where certain persons are simultaneously de-scribed as being incapable of sinning, yet wholly defined by sin because of their participation in cultures whose highest form of individual actualization is sinful social egoism. An instance of this is Niebuhr's discursive construction of *the Negro*, which creates a subject who is at once an inescapable agent of sin by virtue of being embedded within a "primitive/backward" culture and a creature incapable of sinning because of its incapacity to enact the type of agency that Niebuhr identifies as the prerequisite for sin. So the primary flaw in Niebuhr's rhetorical structure is his reliance on seemingly incommensurate descriptions of persons and their relation to sin.

Beyond the logical error, this conflict causes a more profound problem for Niebuhr's doctrine of sin, which is raised by the tendency of traditional Christian theology to position sin as a subset of theological anthropology. Specifically, the tradition has held that sin is an inextricable part of the human condition. If this is true, then the incapacity of certain persons to sin would either render those persons something other than human, or it would conflict with the notion of sin's being a radical part of the human condition. The conflict present in Niebuhr's doctrine is that to make sense of the notion of sin using his schema, one must either deny a measure of the humanity of certain persons or deny sin as a part of the human condition. Either alternative is plainly troublesome to the Christian theologian.

When sin-talk uses negative cultural images in a way that fails to recognize their negative bias, it unwittingly treats these images as if they have the capacity to convey some significant, even self-evident, truth about the persons and communities to which they refer. It thus reinforces and perpetuates harmful stereotypes. This is the problem we saw in Plantinga's use of the *urban predator.* Since all sin-talk is embodied in rhetoric to some extent, the issue is not rhetorical embodiment in and of itself. Rather, the issue is to what extent a theologian embodies sin-talk in such a way that it uses stereotypic language and images that are, in that theologian's particular context, destructive of persons and communities. This situation is particularly problematic when a stated goal of the theologian is to counter the workings of sin in its social dimension with the hope of bringing about more just relationships. Reinhold Niebuhr–a theologian whose life's work was specifically this project–provides a poignant example of the potential harm of unselfconscious sin-talk.

The Heart of the Problem: Incongruent Descriptions of Sin

Niebuhr's problem lies in the presence of two competing trajectories in his work on sin. The first trajectory, which is present in his works *Moral Man and Immoral Society* and *The Nature and Destiny of Man,* traces the movement of sin from individual human frailty to collective social frailty. The primal individual sin replicated in social institutions is, according to Niebuhr, egoism, or the more familiar trait, pride. *Egoism* is the shorthand term Niebuhr uses to refer to the will to power, which he finds evident in the human's encounter with creation. The will to power is the inclination of the human creature to try to subjugate its environment (including other persons) as a means of dealing with the perceived vulnerability that emerges from the its finitude.[6] According to Niebuhr, an acute awareness of this frailty leads the human being to place itself at the center of its existence and, in so doing, to arrogate to its personal reality the false status of ultimate reality. So egoism is the narrow focus on one's own identity and needs to the detriment of the identity and needs of other human beings; it is projecting the self's interest over and against the interest of others. Egoism is sinful because it displaces God as the ultimate reality and denigrates God's creation to simple utility.

For Niebuhr, egoism forms the basis for sinful action in the social realm through injustice.[7] Social sin, then, is derivative of individual sin. So the primal sin of egoism is first realized in individual persons and then actualized in the social formations that these individual persons create. This is the structural logic of Niebuhr's doctrine of sin in its first theoretical form.

Let us now look at the second discursive logic of his doctrine of sin. This competing logic is evident in Niebuhr's many articles and essays that serve as commentaries on his contemporary situation. In these articles, most of which are found in *Christianity and Crisis, The Christian Century,* and *Church and Society,* Niebuhr narrates the movement of sin in the reverse direction from the first logic: He traces the corruption of individuals back to the egoistic social institutions that produce them. Thus, in his work *Children of Darkness and Children of Light,* Niebuhr first talks about systemic issues and then the persons who are corrupted by those systems. What we find in this trajectory is the creation of sinners by sinful structures.

In identifying these competing narratives of sin, I am making it clear that Niebuhr has two distinct ways of talking about sin. The first locates culpability for social sin in the propensity of societies and cultures to reflect their sinful/egoistic creators. The second locates it in the corrupting influences of societies and cultures. One could argue that these two models are not contradictory; rather, they are paradoxically related. Human beings are both agents of sin and victims of it. The underlying narrative approach is the doctrine of the fall that characterizes much of Christian sin-talk, with the first moment focusing on the myth of Adam and the second on the world after the fall. For the paradox argument to vindicate Niebuhr it would have to demon-strate that he uses this schema as a heuristic tool consis-tently in his theological–cultural analysis. It does not, however, and when we look at Niebuhr's treatment of *the Negro*, both of his scenarios fail. Niebuhr's penchant is to provide a description of primitive/backward cultures that does not allow for the type of individual agency or crea-turely freedom that is necessary to successfully use the Adamic portion of the fall schema. We are therefore left with the problem of competing logics in Niebuhr's system.

Signifying *the Negro*

Analysis of Niebuhr's discursive treatment of the "Negro Problem"[8] shows the ways that he relates the categories of individuality and culture to the culturally constructed fig-ure of *the Negro*. His description of individuality, which rep-resents his structural logic, collides with his rendering of *the Negro* and *Negro culture*, which represents his discursive logic.

Disregard for the marginalizing tendencies of cultural figures like *the Negro* have debilitating effects on the theolog-ical engagements of sin in its social dimensions. To demon-strate Niebuhr's, I will describe (1) his concept of the ideal goal to which persons are oriented–individuality, (2) the ways he articulated that sinful social formations work to-ward the annihilation of the individual, and (3) his specific treatment of *the Negro*. The third element of my analysis will demonstrate how Niebuhr's discursive renderings of actual marginalized individuals and their culture construct an environmental determinism regarding sin that his structural rendering of the relationship between the individual and society explicitly disallows, showing his treatment of individuality and *the Negro* to create insoluble contradictions between his structural and discursive logic.

Niebuhr's Individual

The idea of the individual, which Niebuhr outlined most fully in *The Self and the Dramas of History*, can rightly be said to stand at the center of his project. In the individual, Niebuhr finds the fullest expression of human existence, for here he finds the enactment and fulfillment of the human capacity for free and responsible agency. This capacity is also the prerequisite for sin.

The enactment of this agency is rooted in the divine-human relationship. According to Niebuhr, it is the divinely endowed freedom of humanity, and the subsequent human acceptance of responsibility for this freedom, that is the predicate of individuality. It is the "freedom over natural processes."[9] To create this conception of freedom, Niebuhr was drawing upon the modern idea that the hallmark of humanity's uniqueness within creation is that while we are yet finite creatures, our finitude does not determine our existence. Humans are thus able, to an extent, to make of themselves what they will.

> Man is self-determining not only in the sense that
> he transcends natural process in such a way as to
> be able to choose between various alternatives

presented to him by the processes of nature but also in the sense that he transcends himself in such a way that he must choose his total end.[10]

As did most of his contemporaries, notably Paul Tillich, Niebuhr located the authentic divine–human relationship in this freedom.[11] In fact, this notion of the free and responsible individual is for Niebuhr the genius of the Hebraic-Christian tradition.[12] He found that in some religions and philosophical systems, the human creature is either swallowed whole into the workings of nature or alternatively divinized and consequently placed out of right relationship with creation. So the crux of responsible freedom is the esteem in which the "individual" holds itself relative to other persons (this includes God) and the created order.[13]

According to Niebuhr, human beings are created by God as creatures marked by the tension of finitude and freedom. Finitude signifies the historical and material limitedness of human existence, while freedom signifies our capacity to creatively make of ourselves what we will in the context of our finitude. When finitude and freedom are properly balanced, persons can fully enact their individuality. This actualization is the result of the responsible acceptance of freedom by the individual. Thus, although finitude and freedom are important concepts, when it comes to the individual, the notion of responsibility holds pride of place. Individuality functions as a normative description of actualized humanity, whereas the term *individual* applies more generally as a description of all persons who are endowed with agency.

Responsibility in the acceptance of divinely endowed freedom has a number of facets for Niebuhr. The one that concerns us is outlined in his description of the dialogues "in which the self is involved."[14] Here Niebuhr speaks specifically about the individual as a self that is dialogically embedded within creation. It is the self's conduct within these dialogues that determines enactments of responsible freedom or enactments of sin through irresponsibility.

There are three major dialogues that Niebuhr identifies within which the self is embedded. They are (1) the self's dialogue with itself, (2) its dialogue with other selves, and (3) its dialogue with God. Niebuhr characterizes these dialogues such that the dialogues the self carries on with itself and with God are privileged. The dialogue with the self is privileged in that it is the first-order relationship within which the self is involved. It is in this dialogue that the self comes to understand its capacity to transcend the natural processes of creation and, in so doing, is confronted with its freedom.[15] The dialogue with God is privileged because it is in this dialogue that the self finds the ultimate meaning of its existence. So the relationship of these two dialogues can be characterized thus: In the dialogue with itself the self finds the predicate for its actualization; and in the dialogue with God, the self is fully actualized.

In this schema the dialogue between the self and other selves is conditioned by the interplay of the two privileged dialogues. That is to say, although Niebuhr recognizes the impact of the self–other selves dialogue as having a role in the constitution of the self, this dialogue is a second-order one. The self–other selves dialogue is by nature the dialogue within which the self is historically instantiated.[16] Consequently, it is the dialogue in which the self's individuality, which emerges from its encounter with itself and God, is expressed as effective agency. Here Niebuhr does not intend to ignore the biological existence that persons have apart from their interaction with other persons. Rather, he means to highlight the point that it is in the enactment of its human-ity—the enactment of its particular freedom—that the self be-comes involved with the "dramas of history."[17] Thus, while the self is involved with other selves from the moment of its birth, only when the self understands itself to be a self in freedom and responsibility can one rightly say that its dia-logical relationship with other selves begins.[18] Additionally, it is at this point of dialogical realization that the self claims its individuality—that is, the self takes responsibility for its freedom.

The place of these dialogues in Niebuhr's discussion of sin is this: The corruption of the two privileged dialogues has the consequence of rupturing the self–other selves dia-logue. This rupture is materialized as injustice.

> The Bible defines sin in both religious and moral terms. The religious dimension of sin is man's rebellion against God, his effort to usurp the place of God. The moral and social dimension of sin is injustice. The ego [here read self] which falsely makes itself the centre of existence in its pride and will-to-power inevitably subordinates other life to its will and thus does injustice to other life.[19]

So, for Niebuhr, injustice is the concrete instantiation of the self's exaltation of itself over and against the claims of others. He uses the term *pride* to describe this superarroga-tion. This pride is the universal human trait of believing that the human creature, using only its own resources, can prop-erly comprehend and embody perfected human existence. It is visible both in the human collective and in the lives of individual persons. Perfected human existence includes understanding and living in proper relationship to God, the self, and creation.[20] In the self's historical instantiation of pride, Niebuhr finds the irresponsible enactment of freedom, or the enactment of injustice. Here I draw a direct connection between irresponsibly enacted freedom and injustice because in Niebuhr's schema–the dialogical character of human existence–the enactment of the self's freedom necessarily impinges upon the existence of other selves. The enactment of the self's freedom is, therefore, the basis of justice (the accommodation of the self's claims to the rightful claims of other selves) or injustice (the elevation of the self's claims to the detriment of other selves). This rough equivalence between injustice and the irresponsible enactment of individual freedom has as its analogue the workings of injustice in social systems: They enact injustice inasmuch as they ascribe significance to themselves at the expense of individual persons and other communities. For Niebuhr, social systems are never wholly good or bad; rather, they simply seek to preserve themselves, and in so doing function justly or unjustly given the particular circumstance.

The significance of the individual as a category for Niebuhr is twofold. First, in Niebuhr's estimation it is only through the self's appropriation of its unique individuality that a person is able to encounter and be in proper relationship to God.[21] Only in the acceptance of responsible freedom, which is accomplished in the self's appropriation of its individuality, does the self realize that the true measure and meaning of its existence cannot be wholly equated with the finite conditions of that existence. This realization causes the individual to seek the meaning of its existence beyond the immediate conditions of its finitude. For Niebuhr, this search for ultimate meaning inexorably points to God.

> The human spirit in its freedom is finally bound only by the will of God, and the secret of its heart is only fully known and judged by the divine wisdom. This means that human life has an ultimate warrant for transcending the custom of tribes, rational rules of conduct, and all general and abstract norms of behavior. . . . According to the Christian faith, each individual life is subjected to the will of God. It is this obedience to the divine will which establishes the right relation between the human will in its finiteness and the whole world order as ruled by God.[22]

The second point of significance is that only the individual–a self who enacts its responsible freedom by claiming its individuality–who has the resources available to it to transcend any given social formation has the capacity to bring about a modicum of justice in imperfect societies. Through its realization that creaturely existence has a meaning that transcends the conditions of finitude, the creature is freed from the necessity of preserving itself, and, by extension, its social formations, at all costs. Instead, the individual is capable of existing within finitude in a way that honors other individual persons–including God–and enacting justice in its existence. According to Niebuhr, this capacity is unavailable to human societies because the requisite transcendence is a feature of individuality. At their best, human societies can approximate justice, but only because justice is an intuition of the individuals who construct these societies.

It is safe to hazard the prophecy that the dream of per-
petual peace and brotherhood of human society is one
which will never be fully realized. It is a vision
prompted by the conscience and the insight of *individual*
man, but incapable of fulfillment by collective man [who
must] . . . content himself with a more modest goal . . . a
society in which there will be enough justice, and in
which coercion will be sufficiently non-violent to pre-
vent his common enterprise from issuing into complete
disaster.[23]

The individual is a theologically significant category
because it is only in the proper appropriation of individuality that the self can be in right relation to God and to creation. Moreover, it is only through the "conscience and
insight of individual man" that a vision of life beyond the
immediate conditions of finitude is available to human societies. The individual is, thus, the foundation of morality
and justice in the relationships between selves, the relationships that constitute human societies.

The Annihilation of the Individual

The word most often used by Niebuhr to describe sin in its
social dimension is *injustice*. Injustice identifies the historical
instantiation of sin on the level of social formations made
evident in the denial of the proper claims of individuals
within their social context. This denial is always the result of
the exaggerated claims of some within society whose societal power allows them to enforce their claims upon weaker
members of society.[24] While this definition immediately
brings to mind instances of coercive group relations that

result in the social, bodily, or economic harm of less powerful members of society (e.g., the oppression of African
Americans throughout American history), this immediate
intuition should not be mistaken for an adequate portrayal
of Niebuhr's understanding of injustice. In fact, these instances of injustice, which Niebuhr attributes to social egoism, are only the historical effects of what he identifies as
the preeminent sin of which societies are guilty—namely, the
annihilation of the individual. By this Niebuhr means the
cultural and social destruction of the self that renders the
self unable to be in right relationship to God, itself, and
other selves. On my reading of Niebuhr, all historical instantiations of sin in its social dimension are derivative of
this original sin.

This "original" sin is properly understood as the
province of societies. That is to say that the phrase *the annihilation of the individual* serves as a way of talking about the
sinful nature of social formations prior to the historical instantiation of any particular social sin. In this, Niebuhr is
making use of the traditional Christian distinction between
original and actual sin, or between the propensity to sin and
the activity of sin. The notion of the annihilation of the individual is Niebuhr's formal way of speaking about the inclination of societies to ascribe ultimate meaning to
themselves at the expense of individual persons. Specifically, the annihilation of the individual stands for the distortion of the relationships of the individual to God, to itself,
and to other individuals. This complex of relational distortion is expressed in the tendency of societies to either ele-
vate the individual to such an extent that it is no longer an
organic part of creation or, alternatively, to sublimate the
individual within the collective society to the point that the

individual as individual ceases to exist. The terms that Niebuhr employs to speak about these two alternatives are *individualism* and *collectivism*. Though seemingly quite different, these two tendencies produce the same result: Each in its own way incapacitates the individuality of the members of a society. Niebuhr further argues that the consequence of this incapacitation is that the members of a society are left with little recourse but to find ultimate meaning in the society itself. This in turn renders them totally dependent upon the society for the categories and language through which the concepts of ultimate meaning and morality can be expressed.

To appreciate the character of the two ways that societies annihilate the individual, it is necessary to understand both the theological anthropology that undergirds Niebuhr's concept of the individual and the distinct ways that these two destructive patterns work to destroy that individual. The theological anthropology that Niebuhr employs sees in the human person an indivisible unity of body and spirit. The body is the avenue through which the self experiences the contingencies of finitude, while the spirit is the part of the person that transcends any given circumstance of finitude. This vision of human persons understands them to be creatures who, by nature, seek meaning in both the physical and spiritual aspects of their existence. Human beings seek an interpretation of their existence that takes seriously the physical contingencies of their existence and provides an account of reality that adequately transcends the immediate circumstance in which they find themselves. But the societal tendencies toward individualism and collectivism do not adequately meet this dual need of humanity.

Niebuhr identifies individualism and collectivism as political and philosophical ideologies. That is to say, each of these problematic tendencies is expressed both in philosophical movements and in concrete social formations. He outlines the contours of these destructive patterns in *Moral Man and Immoral Society* and *The Nature and Destiny of Man.*

Individualism

Niebuhr provides a complex description of how humanity's egoistic imbalance becomes apparent. Most notably, his description identifies a fundamental denial of the creaturehood of the individual, denying its inherent relatedness to and accountability before God. Individualism denies the body–and–spirit character of human existence in favor of a more limited appeal to rationality (it therefore fails to satisfy the need for an interpretation of human existence that accounts for bodily contingencies with sufficient seriousness). In the first instance of this appeal, the mind or rationality of the human creature is regarded both as the *imago Dei* and as having the capacity to bring about human progress and salvation. In the second instance, there is the false idea that the mind is the creator of human reality and therefore the final arbiter of value and meaning within creation. In both of these denials, Niebuhr contends that the individualistic society engages in a type of idolatry that divinizes the claims of the individual and in so doing obliterates any responsibility to honor the claims of the self's dialogical partners, God and other selves. Niebuhr identifies this evasion of responsibility as the sin of individualism.

Philosophically, Niebuhr argues that undergirding this tendency are systems of thought typically identified as "idealism" or "rationalism." Niebuhr traces this philosophical trajectory back to the ancient Greeks but then argues for its principal emergence in modernity–the period initiated with the Renaissance.[25] He describes it as a system of thought that locates the uniqueness and excellence of humanity in the capacities of the mind. This would mean that humanity's mastery of creation is rooted in the transcendent ability of humanity to think beyond the exigencies and confines of the moment. Politically and socially, Niebuhr finds this tendency evident in societal practices that have an overly high esteem for ideas or value mechanistic and technological advance more than the physical needs of creation. Niebuhr further finds this individualistic pattern problematic because it recognizes no authority beyond mechanistic rationality and therefore denies God. The resulting social ethos is one that interprets creation primarily in terms of its utility for the realization of individualistic aspiration.

Collectivism

The counterpoint to the excesses of individualism is what Niebuhr identifies as the societal tendency toward collectivism, or naturalism.[26] Collectivism sublimates human transcendence and ultimate meaning by linking it too closely with some structure of finitude–some phenomenon that is understood as a feature of the natural workings of creation. Although it may immediately seem that Niebuhr is bringing attention to forms of nature religion (e.g., indigenous spiritualities), he is not. Rather, he is pointing to systems of belief that tend to raise a distinct element of finite creation to the level of ultimate meaning–nationalism, for example. Here Niebuhr identifies the working of a natural phenomenon–the formation of a nation–and then the idolatrous sin that follows when the nation proffers itself to its citizenry as a source of ultimate meaning. "Naturalistic philosophies may (and in modern nationalism do) destroy individuality by emphasizing consanguinity and other natural forces of social uniformity as the only basis of meaning."[27]

Niebuhr further develops his account of naturalism by focusing on social practices that are intended to construct and maintain the collective self. This collective self has two significant characteristics. First, it offers the possibility of achieving personal transcendence through the divinization of some aspect of finitude with which one can totally identify (e.g., ethnicity). It offers the individual self the possibility of being elevated above the mundane (transcending finitude) through participation in the life that the collective self offers.[28] Second, it requires the complete allegiance of the individual members who make up the collective, at least with respect to the facet of finitude that the collective divinizes. This means that while the society allows its members some degree of freedom in expressing their individuality, it does this only within the limits specified by the collective self. Niebuhr has great difficulty with any concrete form of collectivism because it involves the proscription of individuality. By assuming the power to be both the source of ultimate meaning and the arbiter of the individual's self-realization, the collective self (the society) becomes divine.

Beyond the idolatry that Niebuhr identifies, the collective self is problematic because societies cannot move beyond the confines of their own existence and remain mired in the truncated forms of morality and justice that are endemic to simple self-preservation. Consequently, the transcendence that the collective offers the individual is illusory and incapable of meeting the human need for ultimate meaning.

The result is that each tendency toward the annihilation of the individual represents the bent of human societies to usurp the place of God–as the source of ultimate meaning and the object of human responsibility in freedom–and to incapacitate the individual in its response to God.

> The logic of this annihilation can be stated simply. The naturalistic portion of modern culture seeks to reduce the whole dimension of spirit in humans to an undifferentiated "stream of consciousness," if indeed it does not seek to reduce consciousness itself to purely mechanical proportions. Idealism, on the other hand, is interested in spirit as mind, but generally dissipates the distinctive qualities of selfhood in the abstract universalities of mind. Between them the reality of selfhood remains in constant peril.[29]

The effects of this dual transgression by social formations against individuals are significant.

The hallmark of Niebuhr's social theory as it relates to sin is that societies do not have the capacity to transcend themselves. This lack of transcendence is the reason that human societies are incapable of organizing themselves in a moral fashion. Social formations seek to subordinate to themselves every facet of life within them through a combination of coercion and persuasion. As a result, power, and not justice, is the operative force within human societies. While Niebuhr does not deny that in the exercise of power some modicum of justice can be achieved, he contends that its purpose is the well-being of the society. Thus, Niebuhr depicts societies as recognizing the claims of individuals and groups within them only to the extent that these claims can be brought into the service of the society. This is the identity of sin in its social dimension.

The needs and proper ends of the individual and any given social formation may coincide, but they are not the same. As Niebuhr frequently points out in his work, the fulfillment of individuality is the self's responsible enactment of its agency in its dialogues with God and other selves. These dialogues can only happen within the context of the individual's actualization of its freedom. Social formations, on the other hand, find their raison d'être in the perpetuation of their existence. Under these circumstances, individuality can only be expressed if it does not challenge the basic assumption that the society is the source of meaning and fulfillment, which requires that no morality beyond what is beneficial to the society may be permitted. This proscription means that the proper source of morality, and hence justice (the responsible use of freedom in the dialogues with God and neighbor), is usurped. Ultimately, injustice becomes banal; its only variation is the face that it wears.

Though individualism and collectivism represent divergent worldviews, their social consequence is the same—that the "individual who is completely immersed in historical process is naturally forced to accept the moral, political and religious norms which the caprices of that process make definitive at a given moment."[30] These worldviews annihilate the individual by their destruction of the social and cultural transcendence necessary to challenge the regime of knowledge and custom that is operative in any given society at any point in history. Niebuhr's identification of the two destructive modalities of societies moves beyond the simple recognition of their debilitating effects on the individual. His contention is that individualism and collectivism are the two fundamental extremes of human social advancement. In the case of individualism, this annihilation is most often accomplished by an atomization of the self in its responsible freedom. That is to say, the self is disconnected from any relationality to transcendent reality beyond participation in a socially serviceable epistemology. The individualistic, or idealistic, societies are identified by Niebuhr with technically and politically advanced cultures. Niebuhr most closely identifies Western democracies with this tendency.[31] Collectivism embodies this annihilation through its delimitation of the individual's responsibility in freedom to the contours of a particular tribe or nation, over and against creation as a totality. Collectivistic societies on the other hand are generally representative of human cultures that Niebuhr would identify as socially and politically primitive or backward. While Niebuhr does not confine these categories to a fault line between the "white West" and everyone else, his discursive embodiment of these tendencies does come perilously close to this sort of social/racial Manichaeanism. In order to avoid an explicit dualism he makes a distinction between societies and cultures.

Niebuhr does not identify a direct relationship between societies and cultures: A society is not immediately analogous to a culture. Rather, society is an arrangement of political relationships, and culture is the realm of customs, art, and technological acuity. By making this distinction, Niebuhr allows for the presence of multiple cultures within one society and sharp distinctions between the sociopolitical character of a particular social formation (society) and the level of technical and artistic advancement (culture). It is this last point that allows him to label technically advanced cultures as socially primitive (e.g., the Soviet Union) and to identify primitive cultures in socially and politically advanced societies (e.g., *Negro culture* in the United States). Although this strategy may seem to be an attempt at a value–neutral explication of various configurations of human relationships, it is not. At first glance, it may appear that Niebuhr's presentation of these social formations levels the distinction between them in their capacity to annihilate the individual. This is, however, not the case–Niebuhr does put in place a hierarchy of value. Socially and politically advanced cultures at least recognize that there is such a thing as an individual, but primitive cultures do not, making them morally inferior. It is here, in Niebuhr's distinction between advanced and primitive cultures, that we gain entry into the discursive difficulties of his treatment of social sin.

Niebuhr's Conception of *the Negro*

The place of *the Negro* in American society provided the occasion for Niebuhr to speak both about a particular case of injustice and, more generally, about the relationship between morality and cultural advancement. Specifically, he speaks about the unjust treatment of *the Negro* in the United States.

> In a culture that prided itself on its openness and social mobility, the Negro alone was reduced to the status of Medieval serf. In a nation that prided itself on being a melting pot for all the races of men, or rather of Europe, the Negro was prevented by law and by custom from participating in the process.[32]

In Niebuhr's discussion of the Negro Problem, we find the classic elements of what his system of thought would describe as an unjust social arrangement: unequal distribution of power within a complex society; ascription of ultimate significance to an aspect of the natural processes of finitude–in this case, race; denial of the rightful claims of certain marginalized members of the society; and finally, an epistemological and political apparatus that maintains the system of injustice. Thus, in the situation of *the Negro* in the United States, we seemingly find a confirmation of the validity of Niebuhr's systemic analysis of the workings of social sin. Niebuhr's analysis of the Negro Problem clearly identifies the regime of white supremacy[33] as an instance of the workings of pride in social systems.[34] A particular social identity–whiteness–is ascribed ultimate significance in every facet of the society's life and those persons who do not share that identity are brutalized and excluded. The marginalization of *the Negro* in the national life is rightly identified as a clear instance of social egoism. If Niebuhr's analysis of the Negro Problem stopped here its value would be indubitable, but it does not. Niebuhr finds it necessary to go beyond attributing culpability for the workings of social sin to the regime of white supremacy. He goes on to ascribe at least some portion of culpability to the

> cultural backwardness which was occasioned by, and politically sanctioned the oppression experienced by the Negro. . . . The other source of prejudice is the fear of the Negro's cultural backwardness. If we are right in defining this backwardness as cultural rather than biological, it will of course be cured in time by precisely those equal opportunities of education which the constitution and

the Court seek to impose upon the community. But this
fact does not immediately help anxious mothers and fathers in those counties of the South which regard a
common education as a threat to the cultural adequacy
of their children's education.[35]

This aspect of Niebuhr's analysis immediately directs
our attention to a problem in his approach to examining
this particular situation: namely, failing to question the social and cultural appraisals that are produced by the primary agent of social sin in this context–the regime of white
supremacy. Specifically, Niebuhr unselfconsciously mimics
patently racist assumptions about the moral and social capacities of *Negro culture*.

In his partial attribution of the disadvantaged social
position of *the Negro* to "the backwardness of Negro culture,"
Niebuhr uses a very specific rendering of *Negro culture*. This
rendering relies on an interpretation of *Negro culture* like that
found in Gunnar Myrdal's seminal work *An American
Dilemma: The Negro Problem and Modern Democracy*.[36] Myrdal
sought to give both an account of the particular problem
that the subjugated status of *the Negro* caused for a supposedly free society, and a definitive account of the character
and personality of "the Negro and his culture."[37] While
Myrdal does a wide-ranging study, what immediately concerns us is his description of *Negro culture*. This is his description, found under the subheading "The Negro Community
as a Pathological Form of an American Community":

> In practically all its divergences, American Negro culture
> is not something independent of American culture. It is
> a distorted development, or a pathological condition, of

the general American culture. The instability of the
Negro family, the inadequacy of educational facilities for
Negroes, the emotionalism of the Negro church, the in-
sufficiency and unwholesomeness of Negro recreational
activity, the plethora of Negro sociable organizations,
the narrowness of interest of the average Negro, the
provincialism of his political speculation, the high Negro
crime rate, the cultivation of the arts to the neglect of
other fields, superstition, personality difficulties, and
other characteristic traits are mainly forms of social
pathology which, for the most part, are created by the
caste pressures.[38]

In this plethora of deficiencies, there are several that are
of particular interest because they touch upon the issue of
public morality, or sin's manifestation in communal life, and
are referents that Niebuhr uses to make his assessment
about the backwardness of *Negro culture*. They are the instability of the *Negro* family, the unwholesomeness of *Negro*
recreational activities, and the high *Negro* crime rate. Myrdal,
along with many other commentators, contends that the
pathological character of *Negro culture* expresses itself in
moral standards and cultural forms that are at odds with
those of the dominant culture.[39] Given Niebuhr's identification of contemporary American society—specifically, as it reflects white culture—as the epitome of what can be expected
of human society, the endemic divergence of *Negro culture*
from public standards of morality calls into question the
moral capacity of that culture.

Beyond the identification of *Negro culture* as immoral to
the extent that it diverges from the dominant white culture,
Niebuhr also sees the primitive tendencies to sublimate the

individual at work within *Negro culture*, which is evident in his many references to "those talented individuals" who are able to emerge from this otherwise backward culture. In his estimation, only a process of social intervention by the dominant culture would finally break the pathologies endemic to *Negro culture*. Thus, what we have in Niebuhr's treatment of *Negro culture* is a description of a culture permeated by sin in two significant ways: It is pathologically divergent from American public morality and it tends toward the sublimation (and hence annihilation) of the individual through the workings of its pathology. It is important to notice that, in this schema, individuality is only realizable to the extent that persons disentangle themselves from the pathological *Negro culture*. Persons who remain entangled in the culture and its pathology are always in peril of reiterating the pathology and immorality of the culture. Thus, according to Niebuhr's logic, those unemergent souls trapped within the culture are sinners by definition.

In the schema that Niebuhr presents of the relationship between individuality and sociopolitically advanced cultures, individuality–and thus moral agency–is achieved by transcending the ideological structures that societies produce to ascribe ultimate meaning to their finite identities. Individuality allows for moral agency precisely because it represents the individual being in proper dialogue with God, itself, and other selves. In a significant shift from this understanding, individuality for *the Negro* is achieved, according to Niebuhr, by transcending the pathology of *Negro culture*. This shift is significant because what is prescribed to ameliorate the pathology, or backwardness, of *Negro culture* is what will enable it to be more like the dominant (white) culture.

> The Negro was gradually emancipated from his cultural backwardness, partly by the exertions of gifted members of the race who were able to transcend the handicaps of unequal educational opportunities, and partly by the slow development of greater educational opportunities on either a segregated or unsegregated basis.[40]

There is more going on here than simply the cultural imperialism of a regime of racial dictatorship. What Niebuhr is implicitly contending is that effective social transcendence for *the Negro* is possible through the aspiration to a particular type of "advanced" social formation. So the only remedy to the backwardness of *Negro culture*, with its inclinations to pathology and sinfulness, is to be found in a particular aspect of finite reality–American culture of the mid–twentieth century–which appears to fly in the face of Niebuhr's entire system by elevating a historical contingency to the ultimate goal of social transcendence. This consistent dualism is the major discursive flaw in Niebuhr's system.

The dualism in Niebuhr's treatment of sin and social systems is apparent throughout his work. It is evident in his counterpositioning of the following types: idealism and naturalism, individualism and collectivism, advanced cultures and primitive cultures. The difficulty arises from his apparent lack of awareness about how these categories mutually construct one another. He seems unaware also of the hierarchical character of these sets–one member is always subordinated (less evolved, less morally sophisticated) to the other. Niebuhr uses these socially constructed categories that in themselves reiterate the very structures he wishes to critique because he fails to recognize the dualisms implicit in his own discourse. So when he fails to see that *the Negro* of whom he speaks is a figure constructed by the very social and intellectual discourses that he seeks to challenge, he elevates the "tribalist" structures he argues against as the means and the end of social transcendence for *the Negro*. In so doing, he puts in place an idolatry every bit as pernicious as the ones he challenges in the larger culture.

To be fair to Niebuhr, he does recognize the role that racial oppression—segregation, marginalization, and dehumanization—played in the creation of *the Negro community* of his day.[41] What he failed to recognize, however, is that the mythic backward *Negro culture* existed only as a reductive communal figure constructed to explain and legitimate the oppression of a particular community. Put plainly, the seemingly homogenous, one-dimensional *Negro community* that Niebuhr refers to on numerous occasions was a false category in the rhetoric of commentators such as himself; it had no true referent in concrete reality. To be sure, there were large numbers of African Americans in the United States during Niebuhr's era and they did form a significant number of communities; but these persons and their communities were not the pathological shadows that commentators such as Niebuhr and Myrdal suggested they were. There was sufficient scholarship by such theorists as W. E. B. Du Bois, Willis D. Weatherford, and Melville J. Herskovits that at the time amply demonstrated the rich cultural and moral life of African American communities in Niebuhr's day.[42] Clearly, Niebuhr did not understand the nature of the relationship between white American culture and African American culture adequately. He understood the *Negro community* only as a monolithic cultural representation that lived in the minds and the rhetoric of the dominant community.

This misunderstanding is made clear in the constant tendency of Niebuhr, Myrdal, and others to attribute the deficiencies of *Negro culture* to *the Negro's* history of oppression: "The Negroes of this country were once slaves and they are still subject to many forms of disinheritance. For this reason they are still 'inferior' in many capacities and skills that they have not been allowed to acquire."[43] In making this connection, Niebuhr fails to see that the very terms he uses for analyzing *Negro culture* presuppose a pathology. If the starting point for engaging *Negro culture* is the assumption that it has forcefully been excluded from precisely those societal institutions that foster social and political advancement, then it is a tautological step to think that the culture is socially and politically *un*advanced, or backward, because it does not resemble the institutions of cultures assumed to be politically and socially advanced. This tautological step is required by this dualistic schema.

The dualism Niebuhr deploys establishes qualitative distinctions between societies based on a preconceived notion of what actualized human existence is. He begins with the notion that the socially constructed idea of American democracy (limited though it may be) most closely approximates the best social arrangement for the flourishing of human persons. While it may be the case that personal freedom and some meaningful autonomy are necessary components to the social flourishing of persons, it is not the case that they are categorically synonymous with American democracy. Instead, these social characteristics may be inherent in other social arrangements, but were categorically appropriated into the ideological construction of American democracy in Niebuhr's era. His wholesale appropriation of this ideological construction caused his analysis of other

cultures to be predicated upon cultural representations produced by the imperialist discourses of his culture and
placed his own culture at the proximate point of desired
evolution for these backward cultures.

The result of this kind of discursive engagement with
social sin is that inhabitants of marginalized cultures are
placed in a kind of double jeopardy. First, the culture itself,
by the very terms of its formation, interdicts the type of individual transcendence that is necessary for moral agency
and therefore the possibility of justice within society. As we
saw in Niebuhr's portrayal of the *Negro community*, only the
most "talented" members of the community are able to
transcend its pathology–the implication being that they
have resources available to them other than what is provided by their community. Consequently, the less "talented"
persons are morally deficient by virtue of their participation
in the pathology that is the *Negro community*. Put another
way, persons who do not escape *Negro culture* are by definition sinful by virtue of their participation in the immoral activities of the *Negro collective*. Persons who inhabit more
socially and politically advanced cultures are not in the
same situation, according to Niebuhr's schema–they may be
immoral and they may sin, but it is by choice.

Second, the individual transcendence (the predicate for
individuality) that they enact is one that points not to God
and a right relationship to creation, but rather to another
culture–the accomplishment of the "talented" members of
the *Negro community*. So where inhabitants of the socially and
politically advanced culture realize their individuality in a
transcendence of that culture toward God, inhabitants of
the backward culture realize their individuality through
transcendence toward the advanced culture. In essence, the

inhabitants of the backward culture are called to only a proximate relationship to God–one that is mediated through the advanced culture. In essence, the double jeopardy is that members of the *Negro community* are immoral sinners if they do not transcend the pathological *Negro culture*, but they do not generally have the capacity for such transcendence because their culture does not provide them with the possibility for the individuality requisite for moral agency. So Niebuhr's discursive logic of social sin puts members of the *Negro community* in the odd position of being inherently sinners through their cultural location, yet unable to sin because the freedom necessary to offer the opportunity to be irresponsible is unavailable to them by virtue of their cultural location.

The harmful dualisms in Niebuhr's work are related to the troubling aspects of Plantinga's. As with Plantinga, a major difficulty with Niebuhr's logic is that it renders the sins of marginalized persons as having a distinctly different character from the sins of persons they assume to be normative human subjects. Niebuhr, like Plantinga, implicitly establishes a condition of sin endemic to marginalized groups that is apart from the general condition of sin that exists for all of humanity. The problem is not that Niebuhr talks about *the Negro* as a sinner, but rather that he discusses *the Negro's* status as a sinner as being qualitatively different from that of white Americans.

At this point in my discussion of Niebuhr's engagement of social sin, it should be apparent that the structure of his discursive logic is flawed in significant ways. The dualistic framework within which his argument proceeds assumes an ethical and moral hierarchy vis-à-vis differing racial/ethnic communities, which tautologically leads to a diminished evaluation of the moral capacities of groups occupying subordinate places in that hierarchy. Additionally, his discursive rendering of sin as it expresses itself in these hierarchically related cultures relies upon an objectification of persons and communities that portrays them as little more than creatures of discourse (e.g., "the Negro community," "advanced cultures," "backward cultures"). The problem with this type of cultural representation in the rendering of differing societal groups—specifically, minorities being named and defined by the majority—is that it leads to a false identification of ideological assumptions as self-evident truths (e.g., the pathology of *Negro culture*). This is a dangerous proposition because these "self-evident truths" are precisely the conceptual currency that societies depend on in the establishment of institutions and policies that affect the well-being of marginalized members of those societies. As we saw in my analysis of the welfare debate and critique of Plantinga, this flawed approach's dependence on the ideological construction of persons and communities mitigates against its usefulness as a means to interpret and engage sin in its social dimension.

Differentiation from the Feminist Critique

Before turning to the contemporary relevance of my critique of Niebuhr, I believe it is important to distinguish my work from that of two important contemporary theologians: Judith Plaskow and Valerie Saiving. I want to draw this distinction because it is my suspicion that many readers of this work will assume that a critique of Niebuhr's doctrine of sin that emerges from a liberationist perspective will turn on the idea of categorical inclusion. The feminist critique of Niebuhr–that his account of sin overly privileges the position of white males in contemporary Western society by categorically excluding the lives and experiences of women–holds such an important place in contemporary theological discourse that it seems necessary to be explicit about what I am doing and what I am not doing in relation to it.

I am not primarily concerned with categorical exclusion in Niebuhr's discourse of sin, though it is a significant problem. I believe there is another fundamental flaw in Niebuhr's method that has little to do with exclusion. Behind many of the critiques of Niebuhr's work is the seeming presumption that had Niebuhr recognized the experience of more categories of persons, his system would still be serviceable. My argument is that even with a categorical expansion, as needed as it is, Niebuhr's fatal flaw, exposed in his treatment of the Negro, remains–unexamined dependence on socially constructed discursive objects.

I read Niebuhr as depending on discourses whose only function is objectification. I believe that many feminist commentators read his work as being a different type of objectifying discourse–one that does so unreflectively. Hence, they offer the remedial prescription of categorical expansion, where I propose the radical surgery of conceptual excision. We read his work with different eyes. We do, however, converge in this way: Niebuhr's highly restrictive account of human agency in relation to sin is extremely problematic and his use of language and images reiterates the very oppression he critiques with a type of cultural imperialism that should be the bane of every responsible theologian and scholar.

Summary

In the preceding analysis, I have demonstrated a flaw in Niebuhr's treatment of sin in its social dimension: The character of the rhetorical framework he constructs has limited capacity to describe sin as a human problem. Indeed, Niebuhr's discourse depends on destructive discursive economies that are themselves sinful in their marginalizing tendencies. The sinfulness of this framework was seen to be its reliance on a schema that recognizes two classes of subjects: those who are able to claim their humanity vibrantly and those who can aspire to some approximation of that humanity. Nowhere does Niebuhr question the humanity of African Americans; but the logical force of his framework argues for a qualitatively different form of humanity. Niebuhr might well agree with this observation and suggest that it is a sad reality, attributable to effects of the social and economic proscriptions against *the Negro*. Here the power that Niebuhr cedes to the dominant discursive economies becomes clear. If indeed injustice has the absolute power to circumscribe the reality of the oppressed to such an extent that the enactment of their human agency is diminished, then it would seem that injustice has a creative power that we usually reserve for God. Injustice would have the power to create a world unto itself–as would the discourses that propagate it. So Niebuhr's argument implies, if unwittingly, almost absolute environmental determinism except for rare "talented" individuals who transcend their condition. While Niebuhr certainly recognizes the great power of injustice, I do not think he would assent to this conclusion. Unfortunately, this is indeed the logical conclusion of his argument. He implicitly attributes this determining power to injustice and discourse–or perhaps, more exactly, he attributes it to injustice but surrenders it to discourse.

When Niebuhr deploys the figure of *the Negro*, he fails to recognize that image as thoroughly constructed by the systems behind the oppression of African Americans; his use of the figure rationalizes and furthers that oppression because it has an exclusively negative illustrative function. So in this schema, one can talk only about sins against *the Negro* or about the morally determinative backward state of *the Negro*. Using this language, it is impossible to talk about *Negroes* as being moral agents with capacity for actualizing the individuality that Niebuhr so esteems. In contrast to Plantinga's *urban predator*, the superagent of malevolence, Niebuhr's *Negro* is a hapless victim of circumstance who, tragically, can do no other than sin unless extracted from *Negro culture* in order to have any chance of realizing the individuality requisite for justice. Within the discursive world that Niebuhr creates there is no self-actualization before God for *Negroes* as *Negroes*, there is only the hope that they can be lifted out of the mire that is *Negro culture*.

It should be apparent that Niebuhr exemplifies the first model of problematic sin–talk I identified in chapter 1–the irresponsibility/marginalization model. Where chapter 1 (the welfare debate and my critique of Plantinga) specified the workings of this model as it marginalized persons because of voluntaristic irresponsibility, here we have the imputation of inherent irresponsibility. While the renderings may differ in content, they are structurally the same. Each creates an inescapable definition of moral irresponsibility and casts a segment of the population into the liminal space created by that classification. Both variants of this model target a segment of the society that has historically been harmfully characterized by discursive depictions (African Americans).

It may be too much to ask that good Christian folk be continually reflective about the nature and character of the discursive economies that are present in their contexts. It is not too much, though, to insist that they understand how discursive depictions have worked to oppress people and communities in the past, and to avoid contemporary examples that smack of the same rendering. So, if the imputation of inescapable moral irresponsibility were the warrant for a history of oppression (slavery and then segregation in the case of African Americans), concerned Christians should be alerted that the concept somehow authorizes that oppression. This recognition should lead them to challenge that rendering and the system of oppression it supports, rather than giving it legitimacy in a new context. Failure to do this can have serious consequences for the well-being of the persons and communities stigmatized by the depiction. As we shall see in the next chapter, the continual debasement of a people by the imputation of some inescapable moral imperfection can result in assaults against their very survival if the liminal cultural space they inhabit is demonized and deemed expungable by the larger society.

3

DIFFERENCE AS DEFILEMENT

Dietrich Bonhoeffer and the Jewish Question

The purpose of *Do No Harm* is to name discrete instances of the sins of sin-talk. In the previous chapter, I dealt with a sin endemic to the sin-talk of Reinhold Niebuhr: using a marginalizing cultural discourse (*Negro* pathology) to explain and rationalize a situation of oppression. In this chapter, I will deal with sin-talk that has been at best muffled in its engagement of social sin by the legitimacy a theologian can unwittingly give to a cultural common sense that is fundamentally oppressive. My analysis will demonstrate the importance of attention not only to those things we *have* said in our sin-talk, but to those things we *ought* to have said as well.

With the work of Dietrich Bonhoeffer, we are now turning from Niebuhr's rhetorical perpetuation of a social margin to another theologian's essentializing of certain persons into such marginalized status. This chapter will bring attention to a consequence of misreading how sin is being conceptualized and acted upon in a given cultural circumstance. I am identifying further social instances in which the conceptual framework of sin contributes to the "rules of the language game" of a culture, but in which the actual utterance of the word *sin* is absent.[1] My approach to Bonhoeffer's work addresses the work of a theologian whose intervention into a situation of social sin was hampered by his misreading of the way that the category of sin was being invoked in his context. This misapprehension was the result of Bonhoeffer's tacit acceptance of a discursive economy surrounding Jewish difference.[2]

The Church and the Jewish Question: A Limited Response

The particular instance of Bonhoeffer's marginalization by essentialization that I will examine is his critical response to the laws created to exclude Germany's Jewish population from the nation's political, social, and economic life during the early years of the Third Reich. Specifically, I will examine his essay addressing the enactment of the "Restoration of the Professional Civil Service" legislation (which contained the now infamous Aryan clauses) on April 7, 1933.[3] In this essay Bonhoeffer explicitly engages the legislation's intrusion into church matters by its requirement that all persons with more than one-fourth Jewish ancestry be excluded from ecclesial office. In *"Die Kirche vor der Juden Frage"* ("The Church and the Jewish Question), Bonhoeffer argues forcefully against both a litmus test for competency in ministry beyond the discernment of the church and the imposition of church membership requirements extraneous to professing faith and baptism.[4] Bonhoeffer makes a parallel argument against the exclusion of Jews from German public life because of some presumed "essence" that threatened the German way of life.

Bonhoeffer was writing in a context that he thought was just another historical instance of state-sponsored oppression of Jews. He approached the situation, therefore, as one in which the social dimension of sin should be interpreted primarily in terms of the regime's activities. While certainly the policies of the Nazi regime represented a significant social sin, I believe that there was a far more insidious dimension of sin at work in Bonhoeffer's context. The policies that Bonhoeffer stood against represented more than simply political persecution. A sociocultural trajectory that consciously intended to eliminate Jews from the German national life was set in motion by this legislation. Fundamental to this trajectory was the identification of Jewish difference with ontological sin, or defilement. Addressing the social sin in this context required an immediate engagement with this particular notion of Jewish difference, but Bonhoeffer did not accomplish this task.

I believe that a primary reason for this oversight was that Bonhoeffer was so steeped in the discursive economy surrounding Jewish difference that he failed to see how potentially lethal it could be. While it would have been too much to ask for Bonhoeffer to foresee the organized attempt to exterminate German Jews, the Final Solution, I think he should have seen the wholly negative way that Jewish difference was being mediated in his context. Bonhoeffer failed to recognize that, from the outset, he did not have the luxury of nonpartisan language at his disposal;[5] "*der Jude*" (*the Jew*) and its presumed referent–Jewish persons–had an exclusively negative connotation in German communal discourse.[6] Consequently, any unnuanced handling of language and ideas about the Jewish people and Jewish culture would almost certainly have reinforced the basic presupposition that undergirded the Aryan clauses in the first place: Jewish difference and its vocation of contamination.[7]

My analysis of Bonhoeffer will therefore seek first to describe the place of *the Jew* in the cultural context that precipitated the legislation that his piece challenged. Understanding the national project that created this context will help us appreciate why I am interpreting the discursive function of *the Jew* as being embedded within a ritualistic discourse of purification/defilement. An appreciation of the purposes and consequences of the rhetorical rendering of Jews as defiling in their very being is necessary to see how Bonhoeffer's treatment of "the Jewish Question" legitimates the essentialization of Jewish difference while trying to combat the social and legal disabilities that flow from that very notion of difference.[8]

The Mechanics of Utopia

The primary project of the Nazi regime was no less than the creation of a German utopia. By this I mean the creation of a society that was something new and utterly ideal. This society was neither European nor modern, but rather a "pure" society that embodied the transhistorical Germanic spirit.[9] This new society was predicated upon the notion of race at its core. The Third Reich was to be, quite simply, a racial kingdom—an Aryan empire.[10]

Beyond being merely the objective of the Nazi regime, the creation of this Aryan nation became a German national project. The society placed all the significant sectors of its public life–politics, economics, culture, and religion–in the service of this objective. Politically, the Aryanization of the German national life was accomplished by co-opting virtually every essential branch of both civil and governmental organizations. Through the promulgation of exclusionary legislation and economic policies, the German economy was rendered bereft of non-Aryan enterprises.[11] Culturally, the national program of *völkisch* retrieval expunged from the literary, musical, and visual arts landscape any trace of a non-Aryan aesthetic.[12] Finally, through the required participation of all religious communities in verifying the racial ancestry of all citizens and in taking the oath of loyalty, the church was made symbolically and administratively a partner of the Nazi regime in the building of this society.[13] It was through the coordination of these facets of German public life that the Nazi regime sought to systematize the creation of this pure Aryan state. Further, the regime rendered the creation of this state the responsibility of every Aryan citizen. There was no area of German communal life that was not amalgamated into this project.

In establishing this kingdom of race, or Aryan nation, the Nazis were actually creating not simply a new configuration of the customs and mores of contemporary German society, but rather a new order. This new order, while not quite created ex nihilo, was something entirely beyond the mundane. The Third Reich was to be a manifestation in history of a mythical kingdom, whose being was rooted in the destiny of the Aryan *Volk*. That is, this new kingdom–the Third Kingdom–was to be a physical instantiation of the metaphysical kingdom of Germanic spirit and blood. "The state was, therefore, not solely a functional apparatus that could be used or laid aside at will. The state was an emanation of the *Volk*, and the form in which the *Volk* attained to historical reality and spiritual stature."[14]

By using the objective of racial purity in blood and spirit as a central heuristic tool for interpreting the position of the Jewish people in Germany during the Nazi era, we may better understand why it was not enough for the regime to marginalize and segregate the Jewish population in German civic and cultural life. In most historical instances of radical marginalization, exclusion, and oppression it is enough to inflict a "social death" upon the despised group or, at the extreme, to expel the "alien" from "our" midst.[15] Yet in this case the Nazi regime seemed to feel a necessity to extinguish the social and cultural presence of the alien as such—an imperative that the new Germany must be rid of the "influence" of *the Jew*. The Third Reich must be made *Judenfrei*, "free of Jews."

Recognizing that the society being established by the Nazi regime was to be an Aryan utopia requires moving beyond an explanation of Germany's Jewish persecution that rests exclusively on the terms of political or geopolitical expediency—and the attendant explanatory categories of marginalization and exile. While certainly the discursive engagement with the Jewish Question, or the problem of the Jew, during the nascent years of the Nazi era was carried out on a sociopolitical level, the conceptual framework was not primarily concerned with the issues of social formation (e.g., who is a citizen and who is not). Rather, the conceptual framework was ideologically and rhetorically structured to center upon the progenitive project of bringing about this new utopia. Justification for the exclusion of Jews would therefore rely on language that exceeded the merely political to encompass the project's cosmic significance.

The Aryan was the materialization of the blood, the spirit, and the culture of the German people in the cultural discourse of the Nazi regime.[16] In this regard, the Aryan figure symbolized both the aspiration of an emergent people and the realization of a cosmic destiny. In this schema *the Jew* functioned in the communal discourse of the nascent Nazi era as the essential other: the antitype of the Aryan.[17] As with every culturally imposed abstraction, there was little room for distinction between *the Jew* the cultural figure and actual Jewish persons as flesh-and-blood entities. *The Jew* became the antithesis of every aspiration and the cause of every vexation for the Aryan *Volk*.

The Jewish Question became one of metaphysical significance in the cultural consciousness of German society. *The Jew* was not simply a term referring to a racial, religious, or ethnic assignation. Rather, the Jewish presence was understood to be so corrosive that its very existence threatens the destruction of society. This was particularly dangerous in the Nazi milieu because of the heightened significance of the discursively rendered *Volk*. The notion of the Jewish threat cut right to the cosmic existence of the Aryan people.

It is in not challenging this perception of Jews in communal consciousness that Bonhoeffer falters. As the antithesis to the Aryan aspiration, Jewish difference, however it was articulated, had a wholly negative connotation. Beyond cultural discursive economies, *the Jew* carried with it an aspect of defilement. Because German society was in the midst of a ritual enactment of establishing a racial and cultural utopia, the antithesis of that enactment was understood in terms of defilement and corruption. The figure of *the Jew* functioned to represent the central contaminant that threatened the creation of the new society. Whether conceptualized as the Bolshevik or the craven capitalist, *the Jew* was anathema to the creation of the Third Reich. The immutably alien nature of Jewish blood and Jewish substance was bound to its contamination.

Misreading Culture

Bonhoeffer's ideological and rhetorical context was one in which Jews posed a danger to the emergent Aryan nation in cosmic proportions by virtue of being Jews. Jewish blood and spirit, materialized in the objectifying figure of *the Jew*, was antithetical to the very survival of the Aryan nation. While much of the anti-Semitic discourse that emanated from the Nazi regime focused on the "transgressions" of Jews (e.g., a world Jewish conspiracy), the rhetorical assault on the Jews depended primarily upon a metaphysics of race: Jews were not damned for what they had supposedly done, or were doing, but because they were Jewish. In this regard, *the Jew* functioned in Bonhoeffer's context much the way *the Negro* functioned in Niebuhr's. Also, the religious overtones of the rhetoric may have seemed to resemble discursively the particular form of anti-Semitism that characterized the Christian theological tradition in the West, but this instance of anti-Semitism was different. Even though the Western Christian tradition viewed Jews with suspicion and loathing throughout its entire history, the idea that the Jew could be made clean through union with Christ was always kept alive.[18] For example, in 1546 Martin Luther commented that

"We would still show them the Christian doctrine and ask them to turn and accept the Lord whom they should by rights have honoured before we did. . . . Where they repent, leave their usury, and accept Christ, we would gladly regard them as our brothers."[19] In the metaphysics of the Nazi ideology, however, there was no remedy for the uncleanness Jews were assigned.

Bonhoeffer misread the context in which he offered his essay "The Church and the Jewish Question" by understanding the policy assault on the Jews by the Nazi regime to be predicated upon two factors: (1) a particular interpretation of history and legal definitions of citizenship, and (2) a biologistic understanding of difference. Consequently, he engaged the situation as one that could adequately be countered by the refutation of these two perspectives. A structural analysis of his essay makes this apparent.

Bonhoeffer begins "The Church and the Jewish Question" by framing the issue as a problem of the state enacting laws based on racial difference:

> The fact unique in history, that the Jew has been made subject to special laws by the state solely because of the race to which he belongs and quite apart from his religious beliefs, raises two new problems for the theologian, which must be examined separately. What is the church's attitude to this action by the state? And what should the church do as a result of it? That is one question. The other is, what attitude should the church take to its members who are baptised Jews? Both questions can only be answered in the light of a true concept of the church.[20]

Here we see two rhetorical moves on Bonhoeffer's part: rendering the difficulty as an issue of state-sanctioned marginalization and the church's response, and raising the question of the status of baptized Jews within the church.

Bonhoeffer's approach to the first set of questions is to offer an extended thesis on the relationship between the church and the state. The interpretation he offers is grounded in Luther's doctrine of the two kingdoms.[21] Briefly, Luther's doctrine of the two kingdoms holds that the world as Christians understand it consists of two realities: temporal reality (the kingdom of the world) and divine reality (the kingdom of God). The citizenry of the first kingdom are those who are not true believers in Christ and who consequently must have their wickedness controlled. The people who inhabit the kingdom of God are those who accept Christ and consequently conduct their lives in a way that is beneficial to the world. Luther contends that because these two kingdoms coexist in time God puts in place temporal authorities to ensure the maintenance of order within the world. If the world were wholly the kingdom of God this measure would not be necessary. Consequently, people must be protected from the wickedness of themselves and others. This is done by what Luther characterizes as "the law and the sword." In this doctrine Luther echoes both Augustine and Paul. His understanding of the bipartite nature of reality clearly harks back to Augustine's view of creation presented in *The City of God*.[22] Paul's admonition to respect authorities (Rom. 13:1–8) is plainly the inspiration for his understanding of governments and their purpose. A significant piece of Luther's retrieval of this Pauline view of the place of temporal authorities is the belief that the church should not interfere with governments as they work to bring order within society. According to this view, only in the most extreme circumstances is the church warranted to make such interference.[25]

In his reiteration of this doctrine, Bonhoeffer immediately recognizes the state to be God's order of preservation in a godless world. As such, he contends, it should be free from interference by the church in mundane matters. In a step beyond the tradition, Bonhoeffer goes on to say that this principle of noninterference is provisional. It is predicated on the maintenance of law and order by the state.

When Bonhoeffer talks about law and order, he does not rely on a flat understanding of those terms that can be reduced simply to order within society. He imputes a sort of dynamism to their meaning by asking the question: Is there too little law or is there too much? By making this discursive move, Bonhoeffer is implicitly arguing that the church's estimation of the functioning of the state cannot be reduced simply to identifying the presence or the absence of order; it must make its assessment in degrees. Bonhoeffer thus characterizes the relationship between the state and the church as one that assumes the possibility of conflict. Any situation where there is too little law or too much law is a fundamental violation of the relationship.

In the state persecution of Jews, Bonhoeffer finds that both situations exist. In the case of the Jewish community at large, the failure of the government to provide the same protections for Jews as for other citizens indicates that there is too little law. In the state's deliberate exclusion of baptized Jews from church leadership roles, there is too much law.

There would be too little law if any group of subjects were deprived of their rights, too much where the state

intervened in the character of the church and its proclamation, e.g., in the forced exclusion of baptized Jews
from our Christian congregations or in the prohibition
of our mission to the Jews.[24]

So the characterization Bonhoeffer offers of the predicate of
the church–state relationship and the status of Jews as citizens clearly emanates from understanding the crisis as
being rooted in legal distinctions: The crisis exists because
the regime is not doing what it should for Jews and doing
what it should not to the church.

In the second section of the essay we begin to see the
basis for this misreading: Bonhoeffer's acceptance of the discursive economy of Jewish difference. He begins this section,
which he devotes to the status of the "baptized Jew" within
the church, with two assertions: (1) that the church can in no
way accept state interference with the way it deals with its
members, and (2) that the "Jewish problem" has a different
character for the church than it does for the state. In making
these assertions, Bonhoeffer legitimates his earlier challenge
to the state's enactment of too much law and frames the leg-
islative assault on Jews in theological terms. "The Church
cannot allow its actions towards its members to be prescribed by the state. The baptized Jew is a member of our
Church. Thus the Jewish problem is not the same for the
Church as it is for the state."[25] In this statement of the two
parameters for ecclesial discourse about the immediate crisis, there is a point that should not go unnoticed. Bonhoeffer does not discount the presence of a "Jewish problem";
rather, he implies that it is a problem that the church must
wrestle with in a distinct manner. One could simply assume
that Bonhoeffer was using this language to engage the dom-

inant discourse of his time immediately, but I believe it indicates that for Bonhoeffer, there truly was something that
could be called the "Jewish problem."

In the last paragraph of the first section of "The Church
and the Jewish Question," there are several troubling points
in his statement of the relationship of the Jewish people to
the church. According to Bonhoeffer, the church is closely
bound to the Jewish people. It is a bond formed by the es-
chatologically necessary moment of the conversion of Israel
to Christ.

> This consciousness on the part of the Church of the curse
> that bears down upon this people, raises it far above any
> cheap moralising; instead, as it looks at the rejected peo-
> ple, it humbly recognizes itself as a Church continually
> unfaithful to its Lord and looks full of hope to those peo-
> ple of Israel who have come *home*, to those who have
> come to believe in the one true God in Christ, and knows
> itself to be bound to them in brotherhood.[26]

What is immediately apparent is Bonhoeffer's function-
alist view of Israel. Although Bonhoeffer steers clear of the
obviously supersessionist framework used by many of his
contemporaries (e.g., Gerhard Kittel and Paul Althaus), he
does arrogate to the church a special knowledge of Israel
and its destiny—a knowledge Jews do not have themselves![27]
That knowledge is, of course, Israel's function in the future
of the church. That function, which is outlined by Paul in the
epistle to the Romans (chaps. 9–11), is to realize the fulfillment of God's plan with the conversion of Israel to Christ.
Additionally, the suggestion that Israel's suffering is a sign
that God is not finished with this "mysterious people" has

some important implications for the church.[28] Perhaps most significant is the epistemological association of presence and problem in relation to the continued existence of the Jewish community. The very presence of the Jewish community (Israel) is a constant reminder to the church of its unfaithfulness in the failure of its mission to Jews, and their eternal suffering places a continual demand upon the church for succor (a demand Bonhoeffer forcefully points out in this essay).[29] Consequently, the very presence of the Jewish community becomes an affront to the church.

In addition, there is also Bonhoeffer's unfortunate commentary on God's curse upon the Jewish people: "The Church of Christ has never lost sight of the thought that the 'chosen people,' who nailed the redeemer of the world to the cross, must bear the curse for its action through a long history of suffering . . . this people, loved and punished by God."[30] While one could certainly defend Bonhoeffer, as many do, by saying that this particular interpretation of the persecution and oppression of the Jews has a long history in the Western church, this does not change the fact that the practical effect of this rhetorical stance is a rationalization of that history of oppression.[31] The "Jewish problem" was more than an epistemological one for Bonhoeffer.

In the section of his essay where he deals ostensibly with the "baptized Jew," Bonhoeffer takes on the "racist"[32] policies of the German government and the German Christian movement (*Glaubenbewegung "Deutsche Christen"*).[33] His method is to reject the biologistic definition of "the Jew" and by so doing avoid promulgation of the Aryan clauses within the church. Bonhoeffer's dismissal of the biological claim is based on the idea that one becomes a Jew by taking "the

Law upon himself"–the correlative point, of course, being that one ceases to be a Jew when one turns to Christ.[34] Judaism is, then, clearly defined as a religious framework and Jews as believers who live within it. So, for Bonhoeffer, a Jewish Christian becomes a grammatical linkage that cannot be supported theologically and is thus inappropriate in ecclesial discourse. He does, however, make one exception.

Bonhoeffer contends that the church recognizes only one instance in which the term *Jewish Christian* is properly used: to speak of those who would require adherence to some type of law for church membership. Clearly, Bonhoeffer is identifying the *Deutsche Christen* and their allies in the *Deutsche Evangelische Kirche* (German Protestant Church) with the Circumcision Party of the first century. The Circumcision Party was the group described in Acts 15:1–16:5 that went among the Gentile Christians in Galatia and demanded that they be circumcised according to the Law of Moses. The controversy that this activity aroused centered on the question of whether church membership should be governed by some criteria other than a profession of faith. The controversy was resolved in favor of a profession of faith alone, which has been the general posture in mainstream Christianity since. This was particularly the case within the Protestant trajectory with its emphasis on *solo gratia* (salvation by grace). Bonhoeffer thus interpreted the proscription of church office, as outlined in the Civil Service Acts, as being radically unfaithful to the gospel and the Lutheran tradition.[35] His use of this rhetorical device renders the intent and claims of the *Deutsche Christen* movement anathema to the mainstream of Lutheran tradition. It is here that we find the most prophetic moment of the essay–

his uncompromising defense of Jewish converts. Unfortunately, it is here that we also find the ultimately eviscerating effect of his earlier acceptance of the existence of a Jewish Question.

Precisely because Bonhoeffer argued the first section of his essay within a framework that gives legitimacy to the concept of the Jewish problem, he brings to any usage of the expression *Jewish Christianity* a contaminated term. So, when he turns to his discussion of Jewish Christianity, the image he intends–the *Deutsche Christen* and their allies as the modern Circumcision Party–is overshadowed by a more dangerous image of Christianity contaminated by the Jewish "substance." Precisely because he has taken such pain to outline the eschatological dimensions of the problem Judaism poses for the church, any use of the word *Jewish* becomes problematic.

Problematic as well is Bonhoeffer's discussion of the so-called Gentile–Christian Jew. Clearly, Bonhoeffer wants to use this language to distinguish between those whom he accuses of being Jewish Christians–the *Deutsche Christen*–and those of Jewish heritage who have been converted to Gentile (here read "proper") Christianity. As a means of making this distinction, Bonhoeffer contends that the Jewish convert stands no differently within the German church than do the French or the English among them.[36] Plainly, Bonhoeffer is once again trying to undercut the arguments of the *Deutsche Christen* movement. Unfortunately, his comparison of the Gentile–Christian Jew to the English or the French Christian becomes a non sequitur that is more likely to elicit negative connotations of the latter than some positive estimation of the former for two reasons: first, because *Jewish* is such a loaded term throughout the essay, and second, because the

Deutsche Christen movement interpreted the Christianity of the Aryan nation to be something utterly distinct in time. Consequently, a recognition of other ersatz forms of Christianity was pointless. So when Bonhoeffer uses the image of the Gentile–Christian Jew, what comes to mind is someone who is essentially a Jew, in relation to whom the appellation "Christian" is merely a behavioral characteristic. Although I believe Bonhoeffer intends a different image–persons who are simply Christians with Jewish persons in their familial narrative–his treatment of Jewishness to this point lends more credence to the former image. So, within his cultural context, when he speaks about the "baptized Jew" in his closing sentences, his fellow German readers were probably left with this image of a Jew who had gone through the motions of baptism, but remained essentially Jewish.

I would not characterize Bonhoeffer as being a man naive to the situation in which he was living; however, his analysis of the discursive reality he inhabited was flawed. The misdiagnosis that underlies the essay may be attributed to many things, not the least of which was Bonhoeffer's seeming unawareness of the anti–Semitic language loop he was trapped inside. Bonhoeffer would have had to use an exclusively positive discourse that disposed of the idea of Jewish difference entirely to challenge the anti–Semitic presuppositions of the Aryan clauses effectively. In "The Church and the Jewish Question," he did not engage in this type of discourse; he did not say anything positive about Jews as Jews or challenge the fundamental notion of Jewish difference. The consequence of this for Bonhoeffer was that he did not discern the migration of the anti–Semitic polemics and policies of the regime from the historic pogrom model to the new ritualistic cleansing model.

The Multivalence of Difference

In *Race, Nation, Class,* Étienne Balibar provides helpful insights for understanding the seeming naïveté of "The Church and the Jewish Question."[37] Balibar offers the useful point that racism, or, in this case, anti-Semitism, as such, is no one thing, but rather a "total social phenomenon."[38] It is a social system that

> inscribes itself in practices (forms of violence, contempt, intolerance, humiliation and exploitation), in discourses and representations which are so many intellectual elaborations of the phantasm of prophylaxis or segregation (the need to purify the social body, to preserve "one's own" or "our" identity from all forms of mixing, interbreeding, or invasion) and which are articulated around stigmata of otherness (name, skin colour, religious practices).[39]

With this reminder several things become apparent in relation to Bonhoeffer's essay. The first is that his project was challenging a total social system that was in the midst of identity formation through a ritualized cleansing of the nation, not a proper clarification of legal and ecclesial distinctions and relationships. Also, he was seemingly oblivious to the fact that the figure of *the Jew*—the objectified other—over and against which German political, social, and Christian communities might define themselves, was the primary function of the language game in which he contended.

The result of these oversights was predictable: The strategies Bonhoeffer used in his challenge to the Aryan clauses—the rejection of biologistic claims and of "Jewish

Christianity"—were so thoroughly infused with the underlying logic of the clauses that they were incapable of the sort of systemic critique that he thought necessary. The deficiency of these strategies is found not in their intent but in their execution. Clearly, Bonhoeffer intended his rejection of the biologistic argument and his reduction of the difference of Judaism and the Jewish people to culture (e.g., subscription to the Law rather than simply race) to move the issue of difference to a nonessential level. In so doing, he was challenging the notion that there was an essential difference between the so-called Aryan people and the Jewish people who lived in Germany, the notion he assumed to be the basis of the clauses. What was not apparent to Bonhoeffer was the very limited usefulness of these strategies. While they indeed challenged the premises upon which the National Socialists and the *Deutsche Christen* mediated Jewish difference, they did not challenge the operative truism that *the Jew* really was different. In essence, these strategies argued about the form of the proposition, not its material content.

Balibar suggests that there are two distinct ways in which difference in nature is expressed in social discourse. The first, and perhaps the most familiar, is appealing to biological difference.[40] He identifies this conception as the essentialist model. Unquestionably, it was the bias emanating from this model that Bonhoeffer took aim at with his first strategy. The second, much less conspicuous, form of expressing natural difference is the differentialist model. This model expresses difference on the level of culture (e.g., language) and is frequently used to challenge the premises of the essentialist model. Generally, those who engage in this project (Bonhoeffer's second strategy) assume that the

appeal to culture is an effective counter to bias based on biological difference. But Balibar identifies the fallacy of this
assumption: "Culture can also function like a nature, and it
can in particular function as a way of locking individuals
and groups a priori into a genealogy, into a determination
that is immutable and intangible in origin."[41] So the very
recognition of difference in terms of culture can have the
same net effect as essentialist claims about difference because the "genealogy" of culture is so deeply rooted. Culture
is invariably bound up with notions of race and ethnicity.
Thus, an appeal to one in no way guarantees an effective
challenge to the other. In fact, the opposite is probably true:
The two models are mutually reinforcing: culture is derivative of nature and nature is expressed through culture. In
the nascent era of the Nazi regime, this mutuality is apparent in the close connection that its rhetoric made between
culture and spirit—the culture being the historical materialization of the transhistorical Aryan spirit. Here is the nexus
of the contradiction in Bonhoeffer's essay: his deployment
of a cultural figure in an attempt to subvert its own logic.

Bonhoeffer's challenge to the Aryan clauses was particularly problematic because of its cultural objectification of
the Jewish people. With Balibar's insight we are able to see
why this is the case. Bonhoeffer sought to challenge the
racial claims of his opposition by reducing Jewish difference
to the level of culture and religion. What he did not recognize was that these differences could be construed as being
as profoundly essential as biological difference. For Bonhoeffer to have reached the goal he intended for this essay—a
convincing theological challenge to the exclusionary legislation *and* its rationale—he would have had to reject the idea
of Jewish difference altogether. That he did not does not in-

dicate that the task was impossible, only that it required seeing beyond the cultural and theological image of *the Jew*.

Summary

With Bonhoeffer we have a case of what I characterized in chapter 1 as the defilement/essentialization model of sin-talk. As with Niebuhr and the irresponsibility/marginalization model, Bonhoeffer's work is an alternative to that presented in chapter 1. The example I used there, *the homosexual*, was of a deliberate imputation of defilement to a group of persons. Here, we have a case of a presumptive imputation of difference within a context that culturally mediates difference as defilement. That is, Bonhoeffer's context was one in which *the Jew* was a representation of defiling difference, no matter the mediation. Here we learn something important about the defilement/essentialization model of sin-talk. We realize that while a given cultural representation of defilement focused on an outcast group—in this case Jews—may seem the matter at hand, it is frequently only an indicator of a more dangerous issue: namely, the essentialization of the difference that renders a group pariah in the first place. As with the irresponsibility/marginalization model, the representational basis of marginalization becomes inescapable—as do whatever consequences attach to inhabiting that representation. These consequences can be catastrophic.

As with the Holocaust, the Rwandan genocide, the multiple ethnic cleansings in the Balkans, and a host of other tragedies throughout human history, when the peculiar madness descends upon peoples and nations that leads them to believe that their salvation is wrapped up in the erasure of some "alien" groups in their midst, no one is surely immune to the hysteria. The words "Never again" are always mirrored with the quiet prayer "... we hope." What we have also seen in these instances is the inexcusable role that Christian communities in the immediate contexts have played. Be it the nationalisms of the German Protestant and Serbian Orthodox churches, or the tribal and ethnic jingoism of the churches in Rwanda and Burundi, the story is one oft told–the people who have been given a vision beyond caste and nation throw it away for a wretched potage of ethnocentrism and hate.

While not the only one, a major reason for these calamities in the history of the church has been the acceptance and perpetuation of the idea that some marginalized group is forsaken by God and a blight on the life of the people. In my analysis of Bonhoeffer I demonstrated how even the best of intentions can go askew the moment we buy into this language game. Far from being an inoculation against the peculiar madness, sin–talk can be a power tool for its perpetuation. The importance of understanding this last point flows from a simple fact: It will happen again. Human history cannot lead us to suspect otherwise. Human history has taught another lesson as well: When the madness grips a society, good Christian folk can be the leaven in the loaf, like the people of Le Chambon during the Holocaust. We are not fated to be the ones who are the salt that is rubbed into the wound.[42]

4

WISDOM FROM THE TRADITION

A Recovery of the Reformers' Discourse of Sin

A Distinctly Protestant Dilemma

The problem of sin-talk that is rhetorically implicated in the structures of marginalization and exclusion is widespread and persistent, which is apparent from my analysis of Cornelius Plantinga, Reinhold Niebuhr, and Dietrich Bonhoeffer. The endurance of this problem raises the possibility that sin-talk emerging from Reformation trajectories is inherently biased toward discursive economies emanating from the centers of political, economic, and religious power, and consequently reiterates the systems of domination that sustain the relations of power in these contexts. But does sin-talk situated in a Protestant trajectory depend so heavily on the social and religious discourses constructed by the dominant social, economic, and political powers of their context that it is completely incapable of engaging social sin as a systemic phenomenon?

Throughout the twentieth century, many theorists contended that the unique character of the Protestant movement predisposed it to an inordinate esteem of social, political, and economic structures of power. Beginning with Max Weber's seminal work *The Protestant Ethic and the Spirit of Capitalism* in 1906, we find the argument made that the social practices and arrangements most valued by the Protestant movement were precisely those that were gaining ascendancy during the nascent stage of modernity.[1] Weber distinguishes specifically those practices that were touchstones of bourgeois capitalist culture, namely, the compartmentalization of the spiritual life vis-à-vis the public life, work as the center of human existence, profit as virtue, and poverty as a sin. The upshot of this concurrent development was that by the time these social and economic practices became the normative structures of Western society, Protestantism had become so identified with them that one could not speak about the Protestant ethic without immediately referring to the "work ethic." Weber coined the phrase *the spirit of capitalism* to capture the relationship between Protestantism and the socioeconomic development of Western culture in modernity.

This interpretation of the relationship between Protestantism and the structures of social and economic power was further advanced by Ernst Troeltsch in his works *The Social Teaching of the Christian Churches* and *Protestantism and Progress*.[2] While Troeltsch maintains the basic tenets of Weber's argument, he does make an important distinction: Where Weber draws an almost causal link between the ascendancy of Protestantism and the emergence of capitalist bourgeois culture, Troeltsch recognizes a multiplicity of forces at work in the evolution of both of these systems. His analysis leads to a more coincidental account of the simultaneous evolution than a causal one. That is to say, Troeltsch believed that while the social and economic forces that characterized the nascent era of modernity in the West were very compatible with a Protestant worldview, and hence formed a symbiotic relationship with the ascendant movement, they were powerful forces in their own right in the development of the West. Troeltsch's more complex interpretation does not, however, signal a radical break with Weber's thesis. He still agrees with Weber on the fundamental point that the cultural and economic ethos of Protestantism, whether expressed in the Lutheran notion of calling or the Calvinist ideal of work, provided fertile ground for the development of Western bourgeois culture and vice versa.[3]

R. H. Tawney, in his 1926 work *Religion and the Rise of Capitalism*, likewise takes up Weber's thesis but goes a bit further than either Weber or Troeltsch in his analysis of the relationship between Protestantism and bourgeois culture.[4] In Tawney's estimation, the peculiar relationship of the two dominant movements of the Protestant Reformation, Lutheranism and Calvinism, created a cultural climate that was uniquely hospitable to the evolution of bourgeois capitalist culture. He believed that the characteristic traits of the Lutheran and Reformed movements–the former taking a hands–off approach to the emerging social and economic culture and the latter embracing and sacralizing it–enmeshed them in the emerging society in a way that may not have been possible in a purely Catholic culture given Catholicism's predisposition to appropriate culture rather than respond to it.[5]

While certainly there have been theorists who have dissented from the Weberian thesis and its developments, they have been few.[6] What emerged during the twentieth century was a common sense that ties the evolution of Protestantism to that of Western bourgeois culture. This common sense is evident in such works as *Moral Man and Immoral Society*, in which Niebuhr contends that "Protestantism is, on the whole, the religion of the privileged class of Western civilization."[7]

An adequate critique of theologians writing within the cultural context of modern Protestantism cannot blithely condemn them for using the cultural grammar and linguistic forms that emanated from the centers of power within their society. Readers must appreciate that context does matter, both positively and negatively. But if the criticism is being made that particular theologians construct works overly dependent on dominant discursive economies to the detriment of their stated project of engaging social sin, then it must be demonstrated that in their context they could have done otherwise. Thus, in the cases of Plantinga, Niebuhr, and Bonhoeffer, I verified that they indeed fell into traps that were avoidable. Demonstrating this point, however, is not enough. It is also necessary to show that it is possible to engage sin in its social dimension theologically without being immediately co-opted by the discourses of privilege. Given the close connection between the dominant religious and cultural discourses that characterize the social contexts of these theologians, is it possible to engage social sin effectively using the language and ideas of a Reformation trajectory? Or is it finally the case that sin-talk emerging from the Protestant tradition is effectively rendered unproductive or, as Niebuhr would say, hypocritical, by the very character of its pedigree? My task in this chapter is to answer just that question.[8]

The connection, whatever it may be, between theological discourses emerging from Protestant trajectories and bourgeois culture is not such that there are no theological resources to efficaciously engage sin in its social dimension. The tradition, broadly understood, has taken a trajectory that seems to undercut its ability to talk about sin in language other than that of dominant discursive economies, concluding that it is incapable of constructively engaging social sin. I believe, however, that there are adequate resources in the Protestant tradition to both recognize and speak about social sin and the concomitant structures of language and ideas that facilitate it. Moreover, I believe that those resources can be found in the thought of Martin Luther and John Calvin themselves.

I agree with Tawney's assessment that ideas are like children—they have the ability to create their own life; and certainly much of contemporary Western society can be counted as the progeny of these reformers. It is fitting, then, to use Reformation ideas to subvert some of the more destructive tendencies they have led to in contemporary sin-talk. I propose a way that the thought of Luther and Calvin can fund a new set of ideas that can be particularly effective in subverting the discursive structures and logic that characterize contemporary social sin.

My retrieval of Luther and Calvin's thought will have three distinct moments. First, I offer an interpretation of Augustine's doctrine of original sin. This is helpful because his ideas form the foundation of both Luther and Calvin's thinking about sin. Second, I follow this with a statement of how these theologians appropriate that doctrine to argue that sin is definitive of the human condition. Following this I focus on how they believe sin distorts human reason and consequently impairs the capacity of humanity to understand, much less engage, sin as a part of the human condition. Using these two points in the reformers' doctrines of sin, I will suggest an interpretation of their thought that can intervene in the contemporary engagement with social sin that avoids some of the pitfalls that I have identified in the preceding chapters.

Augustine's Doctrine of Sin

Original sin is the idea that through the actions of Adam and Eve in the garden (Genesis 3), all humanity stands, as their heirs, in a distorted relationship to God. While the idea of original sin has a long pedigree within the Christian tradition as a whole, the work of Augustine has had particular significance in the Protestant tradition.[9] According to Augustine, the transgression of the first pair had the significant consequence of tainting all humanity with their sin, which ended humanity's immediate relationship with God.[10] From the moment of Adam and Eve's transgression, the relationship between God and humanity has been mediate because humanity, in its impurity, cannot behold the fullness of God in God's holiness. As a result, humanity stands entirely in the condemnation of God since corruption cannot produce purity.[11] Also a result of the sin of Adam and Eve is the bent of humanity toward pride and idolatry. Related to the first consequence in that the lack of immediacy leads to the search for an apprehensible deity, this second consequence also serves as evidence of the ruptured relationship.

Augustine uses the term *original* because this sin of Adam and Eve has the effect of contaminating all of their progeny—predisposing them to actual sin—and precedes any particular enactment of pride or idolatry by individual persons. According to Augustine, it is because of this hereditary contamination that sin can be said to describe the human condition. As a consequence of this condition, humanity is condemned both to a propensity to act in ways that violate its relationship to God and to stand in God's judgment because of that propensity. This notion of original sin was, until recent years, a normative part of the Christian tradition's account of reality. The doctrinal question has therefore been about how humanity became mired in Adam and Eve's sin; that humanity is implicated is taken for granted.

The idea that sin is a constitutive part of the human condition is a focal point in Augustine's discourse that was later taken up by Luther and Calvin. While this particular linguistic formulation of the human condition may have been foreign to the reformers, the idea to which it points was very familiar to them. Both Luther and Calvin were convinced, based on their reading of Scripture and observation of the world, that sin was an innate part of human existence. Luther frames the matter this way: "Paul so often uses these comprehensive terms, 'all,' 'none,' 'not,' 'never,' 'without' as in: 'they are *all* gone out of the way, there is *none* righteous, *none* that doeth good, no, not one'; '*all* are sinners condemned by the offense of one': all are sinners and condemned by the one sin of Adam."[12] Calvin, a bit more graphically, contends that humanity, spoiled of its "divine array" by sin, has become little more than "an immense mass of deformity."[13] It is clear that for Luther and Calvin any discussion of humanity must be predicated upon the observation that sin is not merely an accidental feature of human existence; it is an enduring part of it. It is this conviction about the pervasiveness of sin that places them squarely in the Augustinian tradition.

For both Luther and Calvin, then, the question about the heredity of sin is not *whether*, but rather *how* sin was passed along to the progeny of Adam and Eve. Each of the Reformers relates the idea to the fall but gives slightly different inflection to the Augustinian read of what comes next. Augustine posits the passage of original sin in the very act of procreation. This point is made by the fairly consistent distinction that he draws between birth in the flesh and birth in the Spirit.

> The guilt of that defect, of which we are speaking, will remain in the carnal offspring of those who have been born again, until it has been washed away in them by the bath of rebirth. Those who are born again do not produce children of the flesh who have been born again, but ones that have been born. And thus they pass on to them, not the result of being born again, but of being born. Therefore, whether one is a guilty non-believer or a believer who has received forgiveness, one produces children who are guilty, not forgiven, just as the seeds of both wild olive trees and domesticated olive trees produce wild olives, not domesticated ones. So too, the first birth holds human beings under the condemnation from which only the second birth sets them free.[14]

Luther's appropriation of Augustine's scheme continues the idea of bodily transmission. While he does recognize that the biblical text uses a myriad of styles of language (e.g., typology and analogy) to refer to the "original" sin and its consequences, Luther settles on the idea that there is actually something that happens in the flesh. This is clear in his position on both the genesis of sin and its incarnation: "This curse is called *peccatum originale*, hereditary sin or natural sin, which we received by nature from our parents in our mother's womb."[15] "From the fall . . . man lost his enlightened reason . . . also man lost the perfections of his body."[16] Clearly, what Luther points to here is an understanding of sin transmitting itself like a hereditary genetic defect. Luther intends this interpretation to preclude any exposition of sin's transmission that hints at voluntarism: By locating sin's propagation in conception, he effectively dispenses with the idea that sin is passed along either through exclusively representative means (Adam as a type) or through what in his estimation is the more pernicious notion–imitation.[17] This allows Luther to accomplish a task important to his project: describing the malady of sin such that God's grace is the only remedy. The bodily interpretation thus provides a description of original sin that precludes the possibility of amelioration through humanly available means.

In his exposition of the propagation of sin Calvin has a similar concern about voluntaristic accounts of sin's transmission. His approach to countering a falsely androcentric understanding of sin gives a nod to the body as the site of sin's transmission, but goes on to give this idea a slightly different spin.[18] Where both Augustine and Luther privilege procreation as the nexus of sin's inheritance, Calvin seems more interested in saying that the inheritance of sin is more a status before God than a genetic deficiency. According to Calvin's interpretation, humanity stands before God as Adam stands before God. That is to say, humanity participates in Adam, in terms of original sin, in the same way that the elect participate in Christ in terms of redemption. Calvin draws a direct line of identity between the participation of humanity with Adam in sin, and with Christ in redemption.

> We must surely hold that Adam was not only the progenitor but, as it were, the root of human nature; and therefore in his corruption mankind deserved to be vitiated. This the apostle makes clear from a comparison of Adam with Christ. "As through one man sin came into the world and through sin death, which spread among all men when all sinned" [Rom. 5:12], thus through Christ's grace righteousness and life are restored to us [Rom. 5:17]. . . . But if it is beyond controversy that Christ's righteousness, and thereby life, are ours by communication, it immediately follows that both were lost in Adam, only to be recovered in Christ; and that sin and death crept in through Adam, only to be abolished through Christ. . . . Here, then, is the relationship between the two: Adam, implicating us in his ruin, destroyed us with himself; but Christ restores us to salvation by his grace.[19]

So what we have in Calvin's interpretation is the idea of participation in similitude, instead of participation by imitation, in terms of both condemnation and salvation. The idea of similitude is Calvin's view that Adam and Christ stand as the surrogates of humanity before God. In these roles respectively, they represent humanity as a whole. Much as an ambassador is the physical representation of a nation or group in its entirety, so Adam and Christ are the embodiment of humanity in eternity. Calvin thus dispenses with the voluntaristic individualism that he finds repugnant in the neo-Pelagian formulations of original sin. In its place he offers an interpretation of original sin that sees humanity as a singularity.

The idea of human voluntarism as a source of, or remedy for, original sin was objectionable to Augustine and the reformers for very specific reasons. In their estimation, the logic of human voluntarism suggests that in the final analysis, humanity has the capacity to choose sin or righteousness. First, they object to this notion because they believe it necessarily leads to a sense of salvific self-sufficiency that is but another guise for pride and another opportunity to trust human judgment above God's judgment. The second basis for their objection lies in the implicit assault upon the sufficiency of God's word and judgment that voluntarism represents. For Luther, this assault took the form of ecclesial proclamation or practices that suggested that some human venue (e.g., the church) could definitively mediate God's grace. Augustine and Calvin find that the notion of voluntarism assails the sovereignty of God by rejecting the idea that God will save whom God will. In place of this recognition of God's sovereignty, the doctrine of human voluntarism states that for God to be just, God must create the conditions in which individual humans can achieve, or reject, the offer of salvation. In sum, God must respect the autonomy of humanity in a way that humanity is not bound to respect God's autonomy. The way Luther and Calvin saw it, a doctrine of voluntarism led ultimately to a reenactment of the fall.

In my restatement of Luther and Calvin's positions, it is apparent that they do not offer the same description of the transmission of sin. It should be equally apparent, though, that they do share with Augustine a commitment to the principal dogma encapsulated in the doctrine of original sin, namely, that the taint of sin affects *all* humanity. So, whether we express it typologically or biologically, the underlying notion of the participation of all humanity in this condition remains untouched. Further, it is with the idea of participation that we find the first corrective resource for addressing two of the flaws that I have highlighted in some more recent theologians' engagement with sin in its social dimension. These two flaws are the discursive creation of a hierarchy of sinners and the subtextual assertion of ontological difference present in many theological expositions of sin, as illustrated by the irresponsibility/marginalization and defilement/essentialization models.

The Principle of Participation

The principle of participation is, stated simply, the article of faith that *all* humanity (living, dead, and yet unborn) stands marked by sin before God. The idea of participation can counter theologians' tendency to create a unique margin of sinners who are more deeply marked by sin than other human beings by its fundamental denial of any hierarchical depiction of sin as it functions in communities or other categories of society: if *all* humanity stands before God as tainted equally by the sin of Adam and Eve, certain persons or communities cannot stand before God in qualitatively different conditions of sin. This acts as an important corrective to Plantinga and Niebuhr because both, in their engagement with caricatures of marginalized communities, speak about sin within those communities as a state of being. Their deployment of images is such that the persons of whom they speak cannot do other than sin because their communities (unaided) can produce none other than these examples of sinners–a characteristic that neither theologian consistently attributes to the dominant society!

Luther and Calvin were not naive. Both recognized that there exist differing actualizations of sin within human existence; but these do not, for them, form subsequent conditions of sin apart from the universal condition or predisposition. This point is an outgrowth of the traditional distinction within Christian theology between original sin and actual sin. One speaks of sin as a condition, the other of sin as discrete acts by persons and social formations. Put another way, one category is expressive of the evidence of sin–brokenness and destruction within creation–while the other is concerned with a qualitative character of human being. In essence, sin as a condition is not an existential assessment of the state of human affairs. Nor is it a human condition discernible through sociological analysis. Sin is a human condition because all humanity, with none excluded, was tainted in the eyes of God by the transgression of Adam and Eve. Hence, we have the idea of participation. Sin is therefore not a category that can be used to make relative judgments about differing social configurations. Sin permeates the human condition.

The idea of participation can be a remedy to the error of confusing the categories of original sin and actual sin. What was apparent in the work of Plantinga and Niebuhr was that each, in his engagement with the purportedly sinful practices of marginalized communities, deployed a structural discourse of sin as a unique state of being for these communities. They made this error because they relied on a discursive economy in which pathology was the operative social idiom for speaking about these subjects. In his own way, each theologian fashioned this common sense of communal pathology into his discourse of sin as an accumulative condition. Retrieving the discursive link between sin and participation would disallow this type of error by unmasking it as the reinforcement of cultural oppression.

The notion of participation can serve a corrective function in its capacity to make nonsense of the idea of immutable difference that is precipitated by a people's "peculiar" sin. That is to say, it militates against any articulation of sin suggesting that certain persons stand in an atypical relation to God because of some sin that may have been enacted by a community of which they are a part.[20] Likewise, the idea of participation can be used as a corrective to the fashionable fallacy of ontological difference. While difference has emerged within the last few decades as a significant category for use as an analytic tool of social theory, its other vocation cannot be overlooked. The idea of difference is a central underpinning of oppressive economies—both discursive and material. The notion of idealized and ontological difference is used frequently as a means to rationalize the relative positions of power that differing groups and persons hold within society.[21] Beyond this expected use of the notion of difference as a rationale for systemic inequity, the idea of difference can also be used to give currency to genocidal political and cultural regimes, as is amply illustrated within Bonhoeffer's context. Minimally, the category of participation cuts against any simplistic Christian theological justification for this more predacious cultural functioning of the idea of difference. It accomplishes this subversion by the approach it takes to describing the heredity of sin.

In keeping with the Reformation trajectory, I propose an exposition of the scriptural commentary on the heredity of sin that draws upon Paul's interpretation in Romans 5:12–that there is a one-to-one correspondence between Adam and Christ, that one corrupts while the other saves. Using the interpretation of Paul, we come to the conclusion that the relationship of humanity to God, in terms of sin, is not a direct one. Rather, it is a relationship mediated through the two humans who stand in immediate relationship to God, Adam and Christ. Humanity does not stand before God as this one or that one, but rather we stand before God as sinners inasmuch as we are a part of Adam, and as redeemed inasmuch as we are a part of Christ. This rendition of the human proximity to Christ in regard to sin is based on the idea that while persons and communities enact sin to varying degrees, these enactments do not predicate their proximity to God. The idea of participation thus subverts destructive sociocultural articulations of essential difference in a fashion similar to the way that it does the notion of differing conditions of sin.

This is an important corrective, for it is regrettably the case that while the putative conviction of much of the Christian tradition has been that "we are all sinners before God," this conviction has not always played out in theological practice. It has more often been the practice that the sins of those persons and communities held in disrepute within a given social context have received a different sort of scrutiny than have the sins of the powerful segments within the same society. A notion of difference has often played a role in this type of practice, and the idea of participation can effectively act as a counter to this situation.

To summarize, the notion of participation serves two corrective functions for problematic theological discourses of sin. First, it can effectively counter the tendency of some theological expositions of sin to promulgate the idea that distinctions can be made in the condition of sin. In the work of Plantinga and Niebuhr, sin was imputed to stereotypical figures (*urban predator* and *the Negro*) in a peculiar way by their location in a particular community. This imputation of sin stood apart from any condition that the real persons assigned these caricatures might find themselves in as a result of being human. It is this condition—imputed by communal association—that the idea of participation subverts.

Lest it seem that I am making too much of the power of the *idea* of participation, let me assert that ideas are the imaginative currency that give meaning to our world and our interactions within it. We formulate our sense of ourselves, of others, and about our respective places in creation based on the ideas that structure our worldviews and our convictions. So, if theologians, pastors, or laypeople work with ideas about humanity that imagine qualitative distinctions between us, it is a short step for them to then assign theological significance and cultural importance to those differences. This short step can also lead, as we have seen, to the participation of these good Christian folk in systems of heinous oppression and deadly marginalization. A commitment to the idea of participation can have an equal, if not greater, power to motivate good Christian folk to challenge such systems. This is accomplished by the cultivation of a commitment to resist any type of ideological or theological convention that would deny the essential unity of all humanity. My presumption is that the idea precedes the conviction, which precedes the motivation to action. What I am proposing with the idea of participation is the foundation for a conviction about humanity that not only influences, but structures and forms, a basis of accountability for any Christian engagement with social sin, discursively or otherwise.

The scheme that emerges from a Reformation trajectory also militates against the legitimation of difference such that certain predispositions toward sin are ontologically worse than others. It thus counters the idea that the difference certain persons and communities are depicted as representing is of ontological and cosmic significance. In recognizing sin as universal, qualitative distinctions between the human conditions of various communities are disallowed. In fact, the idea of participation has the capacity to expose theological accounts that recognize these differences as being little more than rationalizations for particular power relations within a given context.

Let me offer an example of the type of cultural/theological discourse about social sin that is refuted by this commitment to a singular condition. It is not unusual for a commentator to view news reports about sinful happenings within a poor community (e.g., gang activity) and begin to fulminate that this is but an example of the sorry state of life and morality in these communities. We saw this in chapter 1 with Plantinga and Mead. These same commentators do not, however, use the same measure when commenting about the excesses of the moneyed classes. If they comment at all about the about the destruction and ruin brought about by personal and corporate greed and corruption (e.g., the thousands of lives devastated by corporate raiders in the 1980s and by corrupt corporate management in the 1990s and beyond), it is usually to notice the despicable behavior of an individual or small group of individuals. There is no extension made to include CEOs or financiers, as such, in the pronouncement of sin. So, in one case all are tarred by the same brush (sin as a condition of the community) and in the other fine strokes with cotton swab are made (sin as a condition created by the individual). This is, of course, the sacred cow assumption of upper-class moralists that poverty somehow eclipses the moral capacity of human beings in a way that money and possessions do not. Needless to say, these moralists are rarely poor, or identified as a part of the "underclass" or as "trailer trash." No, the place in which they sit to make their pious pronouncements is usually one that benefits greatly from the current relations of economic and political power. This type of self-serving sin-talk is what a commitment to the principle of participation exposes and contests.

How Can a Crooked Man Know That He Is Bent?

A second helpful point drawn from Augustine's doctrine of sin and taken up by Luther and Calvin is his contention that sin distorts the very capacity of humans to know the good, much less to do it. In the *Retractions* Augustine says it thus: ". . . unless the will is freed by the grace of God from the bondage through which it has become a slave of sin, and unless it obtains aid in conquering its vices, mortal man cannot live rightly and piously."[22] Beyond a simple recognition of the pervasiveness of sin within humanity, Augustine asserts that sin distorts the very capacity of the will to interpret and respond to God's will in creation. Given that his conception of the will encompassed the rational faculties of humanity, it is wholly appropriate to infer that Augustine questioned whether humans could even "think straight" in matters having to do with God and sin.

In phrasing strikingly similar to Augustine's Luther contends: "With regard to God, and in all that bears on salvation or damnation, [humanity] has no 'free-will.'"[23] Clearly, we can also infer that Luther questions the capacity of humanity to interpret reality because of the bonds of sin. I think this is what Luther was saying in his oft-quoted dictum to "sin, and sin boldly." With a bit of rhetorical flourish, he was counseling against the vain belief that it is in our power not to sin. So, excessive worry about avoiding sin was, beyond the arrogance of the idea, a waste of perfectly good life. What Luther may have had in mind was just this: Know that it is not in your power to live a sinless life, and be thankful that God will accept you in spite of that.

Calvin presses this point farther than Augustine or Luther. He contends that the depravity of humanity is total, and in so doing encapsulates a major intent of the doctrine of original sin–that sin is not something that can be thought out of or worked through. With this contention, I believe he captures the sensibilities expressed by Augustine and Luther. It is in identifying this intent and its implications that we find the second corrective resource for problematic sin-talk.

In my initial assessment of Plantinga, Niebuhr, and Bonhoeffer, I explicitly pointed out that they were not intentionally trying to sustain structures of marginalization through their unwitting use of destructive discourses.

Rather, their problem was rooted in a seeming inability to see beyond the "common sense" of their particular contexts. We can draw two observations from the preceding discussion of the doctrine of original sin that are relevant to this inability. First, humanity is given to a false assessment of the extent to which sin characterizes our existence. And second, there is no part of the human person left uncorrupted by sin. The first point speaks to human arrogance and the second to human blindness to the ubiquity of sin. The force of these observations in this discussion is this: Each of the theologians in question seemingly forgot how his assessments about, and prescriptions for, social sin were susceptible to being corrupted by sin. That is to say, Plantinga, Niebuhr, and Bonhoeffer were inattentive to the capacity of their sin-talk itself to be a venue for the reiteration of sin.

These observations about the ubiquity of sin are helpful for reminding us that our meditations on social sin will likely be corrupted by the arrogance of a false and misplaced sense of objectivity and by our initial incapacity to see or fully appreciate the way our language reflects what may be sinful relations of power within our context. In the first instance, it is highly probable that our assessments of persons and communities about whom we are only liminally aware will be thoroughly conditioned by the way those persons and communities are constructed in the public discourses of our society. Plantinga's commentary on rap music is a striking instance of a theologian who exhibits an astounding ignorance of his subject matter but who conveys an extreme level of comfort in rendering judgments. This violation of scholarly method is, in my estimation, rooted in the arrogance of Plantinga's apparent belief that he could write about a musical form that emerges from a culturally despised community without first becoming familiar with that community beyond the images manufactured by the culture that propagated the disdain in the first place.

In relation to Niebuhr and Bonhoeffer, the second observation is particularly apropos. Both of these theologians would have done well to assess the way that the objects of their discourse lived discursively within the dominant culture. Both *the Negro* and *the Jew* were discursive references to persons who inhabited unique places of disdain within their societies. As linguistic figures they represented discursive economies that had coalesced to buttress this cultural disdain. Consequently, the figures themselves reflected and reiterated social relations fundamentally predicated on marginalization and exclusion. In other words, language in general surrounding *the Negro* and *the Jew* served primarily to rationalize social sin. Thus, failure to evaluate the sinful aspects of their own concepts and language critically led Niebuhr and Bonhoeffer to participate rhetorically in the marginalization and exclusion that these figures legitimized.

So, a second way that a retrieval of Luther and Calvin's thoughts on sin is helpful in avoiding the pitfalls I have identified is by exposing as arrogance the belief that we can objectively view and talk about social sin.[24] It helps us be mindful of the probability that our language will reflect the sin that permeates the systemic social relations in our context. For example, even though we may not consider ourselves racist, we do well to remember that our context is permeated by assumptions about race that are rooted in a long history of marginalization and oppression. Precisely because it means something to be white in America as opposed to being black in America, great care is called for when we ponder how sin is at work when the idiom is race. Also, an awareness that particular discursive economies are always at work to legitimize fundamentally sinful social relations should give us pause when we encounter cultural figures that provide simplistic depictions of marginalized communities and their cultures. Accordingly, when a theologian deploys a term like *urban tough* without qualification or explanation, that theologian should seriously examine the discursive economies at work that make the phrase commonsensical. Theologians need to be exegetes not only of Scripture and tradition, but of their cultural and linguistic context as well!

I am not suggesting, of course, that increased attention to context can get us totally out of the mess of participating in sinful systems in our sin-talk. Instead, while we are never wholly free from tainted implication, there are ways that we can minimize the damage that we can see. Certainly, there will always be blind spots, sometimes big ones, but that recognition does not excuse responsible Christian theologians from caring enough about the consequences of their sin-talk to exercise caution when talking about sin.

Summary

In this chapter, I have offered a retrieval and interpretation of Augustine, Martin Luther, and John Calvin's approaches to sin-talk that can counter the problematic tendencies I have identified in the works of Cornelius Plantinga, Reinhold Niebuhr, and Dietrich Bonhoeffer. My interpretation has identified two points in Luther and Calvin's sin-talk that are helpful correctives: the idea of participation and the recognition of the ubiquity of sin. The notion of participation militates against articulations of sin that rhetorically construct conditions of sin apart from the general human condition of sin. This corrective is particularly useful in deconstructing cultural discourses that portray the sins of the marginalized as being utterly distinct. Also, it rejects any interpretation of essential difference that is mediated through or related to sin.

The point about the pervasiveness of sin provides a cautionary note to any theologians who believe that they are insulated from the cultural and systemic biases that might permeate their context. The arrogance that masquerades as objectivity is exposed to be a false estimation by humanity of its own capacities. Additionally, the contention that no part of us is uncorrupted by sin is a forceful reminder that the linguistic and cultural forms that emanate from us are not impervious to this corruption. Our language and cultural forms *do* reflect sinful relations of power that exist within our context.

My interpretation of Luther and Calvin's approach to sin–talk provides an answer to the question with which I began, namely, does sin–talk situated in a Protestant trajectory depend so heavily on the social and religious discourses constructed by the dominant social, economic, and political powers of their context that they are incapable of engaging social sin as a systemic phenomenon? The answer is that while Protestant sin–talk does have the propensity to be co-opted by dominant discursive economies because of the particular religious and socioeconomic history of the tradition, this co-option can be resisted.

5

REDEEMING SIN-TALK

I have sought to highlight the unfortunate practice by many contemporary theologians of deploying sin-talk (theoretical and functional doctrines of sin) that trades in images and language that are destructive of marginalized persons and communities in these theologians' contexts. We have seen how inattention to the discursive economies at work in these sociocultural contexts reflects these economies in harmful ways in their sin-talk. This seeming unawareness significantly compromises these theologians' engagements with sin in its social dimension.

The rhetorical participation of these theologians in oppressive systems and marginalizing discourses is not born of a particular malice harbored by these writers toward those marginalized within their societies. In fact, in two cases they apparently believed that they were being sympathetic to the marginalized persons about whom they were writing (Niebuhr and African Americans, and Bonhoeffer and Jews). Nonetheless, for the theologians discussed, the effect of their sin-talk is to legitimate cultural "common sense" that primarily functions to buttress systems of social, religious, and political oppression.

In my analysis of Plantinga and Niebuhr, I illustrated results arising from two discrete instances of a theologian's unexamined use of cultural and rhetorical figures to exemplify his sin-talk. The primary consequences that I identified were that the sin-talk of these theologians participates in (1) the discursive legitimization of oppressive social, economic, and political systems, and (2) the abstraction of marginalized persons and communities into exotic, pathological monoliths. To use the language deployed earlier, the sin-talk of Plantinga and Niebuhr rhetorically constructs social and cultural margins and then essentializes oppressed persons and communities into those margins. Neither of these practices is a fitting aim or method for a Christian theologian concerned about engaging sin in its social dimension.

In identifying these problematic tendencies in the works of Plantinga and Niebuhr, I sought to make the further point that to the extent that both theologians use and thereby legitimate stereotypic figures, they are denying the full humanity of the persons to whom these figures putatively refer. This denial is always the consequence of objectifying persons and their communities because it does not allow for the type of "thick" account of existence that is necessary for a true rendering of human experience. This denial has serious implications for other aspects of the discourse of these theologians. An area that is immediately affected is, of course, theological anthropology. The first implication is made evident in the recognition that stereotyping persons and rendering their communities as monolithic denies those persons the elements of identity and subjectivity that have been identified in modernity–both philosophically and theologically–as hallmarks of human uniqueness within creation.[1]

The denial of personal identity and subjectivity has the second implication of discursively distorting the theological description of human agency as a venue for responsive relatedness to God. A failure to recognize the individuality of persons precludes the further recognition of their response in freedom to God. This is an important consequence because much of the Protestant tradition holds that it is precisely in our response to God as *free individuals* that we are responsibly claiming our creaturehood.[2] Indeed, the capacity to do more than simply respond to our environment by instinct or conditioning is the facet of our being that much of the tradition describes as the *imago Dei* in humanity.[3] This capacity–which is most often identified in the tradition as free will–is the font of both positive response to God (love and the pursuit of justice) and negative (sin).[4] Because it is an integral part of the Christian account of humanity, any circumscription of the capacity for free will diminishes the humanity of those persons so set apart. Thus, to the extent that persons are rhetorically constructed, as they are by Niebuhr, without a full and robust capacity for free will and agency, they are depicted as less than fully human. Correlatively, to posit some sort of unique propensity to sin, or a distinct condition of sin apart from the general human condition of sin, as Plantinga does, is to participate in the denial of full humanity to persons thus circumscribed. Obviously, this is

not what Plantinga or Niebuhr intended; but these are un-
avoidable consequences of the weaknesses in their work.

In my analysis of the work of Dietrich Bonhoeffer, my
concern was to demonstrate how accepting a discursive
economy surrounding a type of difference can blind theologians to the potentially dangerous mediation of that difference in their particular contexts. Specifically, I demonstrated
how Bonhoeffer's acceptance of the idea of Jewish difference
impeded him from seeing that the category itself was being
rendered as defilement in the midst of a ritual purification
by his society, and, thus, treated as a presence that must be
eradicated. I argued that a keener awareness of the character of this cultural enactment, which was exemplified in the
Aryan clauses, might have helped Bonhoeffer to see the potentially lethal material consequences of this cultural designation for Jewish persons and communities. This was a case
of a cultural response to sin expressed as defilement going
unrecognized by a theologian who was ostensibly writing
on behalf of those stigmatized in this cultural enactment.

Bonhoeffer's oversight was closely related to his un-
questioned acceptance of the notion of essential Jewish difference. While he rejected biological explanations of this
difference, he was entirely caught up in Christian anti-
Semitism, which did not allow him to see that the theological significance that he attributed to the distinctiveness of
"Israel before God" was every bit as essentializing as claims
rooted in genealogy. In order to accomplish the type of intervention he desired, he would have had to (1) recognize
the absolutely defiling way in which Jewish difference was
being mediated in his context, and (2) challenge the notion
of Jewish difference in any form in which it could be essen-

tialized. Because he did not do this, he trapped himself in the same anti-Semitic language loop that the Nazi regime was using as currency for its project, and legitimated the notion of essential Jewish difference.

The difficulties that I identified in the works of Plantinga, Niebuhr, and Bonhoeffer raised the question of whether sin-talk that emerges from a Protestant trajectory necessarily privileges discursive economies produced by the centers of social, economic, and political power and is thus unable to address social sin adequately. While there may exist a propensity within the tradition to privilege these discursive economies, it is not inevitable, which becomes apparent in my interpretation of Augustine, Martin Luther, and John Calvin. As a way to confirm this assessment, I identified two specific resources in the Augustinian tradition on sin that counter the co-option of Christian sin-talk by destructive discursive economies.

The first resource was the concept of participation. Here I interpreted Augustine, Luther, and Calvin, whose assertion of our participation in Adam as analogous to our being saved in Christ does not allow the problematic practices in the works of Plantinga, Niebuhr, and Bonhoeffer. The first of these practices is any mediation of sin that discursively creates *unique* conditions of sin beyond the *general* human condition of sin. A discourse of participation precludes the establishment of a hierarchy of sinners by emphasizing our "equality in sinfulness" in the eyes of God. The second practice is any interpretation of sin that validates an essentialized difference related to or emanating from sin, whether this difference is mediated in biological or cultural terms. Maintaining awareness of this concept of participation subverts the functioning of the discursive economies that reiterate social marginalization through, or explain it by appeals to, essentialized difference.

The principle of participation serves also to remind us of the essential unity of all humanity—first in Adam and now in Christ. This reminder subverts what is perhaps the most destructive outcome of social sin and problematic sin-talk: denying the humanity of marginalized persons. Also, this principle effectively challenges, and, one hopes, overthrows, the long-standing practice of rationalizing oppression, exclusion, and eradication by appeals to the aberrant humanity we assign to our enemies.

The second resource that I found in the Protestant tradition was its insistence on recognizing the overesteem that humanity has for its own moral capacities. This reminder cuts against the propensity of theologians to believe blithely that there is a point of objectivity from which they can assess the full contours of social sin at work. It makes plain the reality that our sin-talk is corrupted by the sin that is at work in our social context—whatever its character may be. Cognizance of this reality may persuade theologians that responsible reflection requires more than a perusal of the headlines. Responsible reflection requires that we interrogate the cultural common senses, ideas, and beliefs at work in our contexts, and assess the material relations of power that underlie them.

Before naming the discrete practices that can help to redeem Christian sin-talk to be prophetic proclamation in the public square, let me reiterate the importance of this project. I have spent the previous chapters describing the conceptual difficulties present in much contemporary social sin-talk. Let me again call attention to the conviction that underlies this entire work: wrong headed sin-talk deployed in the public square has destructive effects on the lives of flesh-and-blood human beings.

Recall my presentation in chapter 1 about how sin-talk was used in the recent welfare debates. For a moment, let us ask what is really at stake in this social debate and the consequences of sin-talk gone askew. First, let us be clear: Christian moralizing played a significant role in the unfolding of that debate. Sin-talk was, and is, implicated in these discussions—more often than not, in an unhelpful way. Notwithstanding the fact that commentators like Mead focus almost all of their attention on the behavior of adults, the primary beneficiaries of welfare (or Aid to Families with Dependent Children, as it was once known) are the most vulnerable people in our society—poor children. These are the ones who suffer most when draconian measures are taken to teach "moral turpitude" and the "work ethic" to poor adults. From my experience in working with the socially and economically vulnerable (I directed an inner-city crisis intervention program for three years), I know that many families are never more than a hairsbreadth away from hunger and a day or two from homelessness. I also know that each worry-fraught mother has a name, and each hungry child a face. These human dimensions are erased by discursive representation: the *welfare queen* and her scion. That erasure makes it possible for nonsense like Mead's suggestion that the poor accept the system that maintains their poverty as something "fine as gold" to seem something more altruistic than the callous, classist condescension that it is. One wonders whether a hungry child or a homeless family would qualify as "the least of these" for moralists like Mead.

While this example is focused on a recent debate, the issues I raise with it are perennial ones facing human society. The distribution of resources, the claim that persons have on the wealth of their society, and the extent to which segments of the population can be cast aside are quandaries as old as human society itself. So also are the questions that face Christians within these societies: Where do we look for sin in our social setting? How do we name it? What kind of difference should our sin-talk make?

What I hope to do with this example, and the others used throughout the book, is to show how knee-jerk agreement by Christians with the cultural assignment of others to a liminal space of marginalization is finally nothing more than baptizing oppression in their contexts. Further, I am trying to illustrate the way that this unreflective agreement leads to a callousness of spirit that deadens the sense of empathy and compassion for the weak. I define callousness of spirit as the rationalization of human suffering in a way that either ignores or furthers the suffering of others. This callousness often evidences itself in the relegation of those who suffer to the inescapable identity of sinner. So, whether it is the person whose body and life are wasting away because of HIV/AIDS, or the child who is doomed to a life of poor education and want, or the "urban tough" whose life expectancy is twenty-five years, the response is always the same: "Repent sinner! Repent!" And when the reply to this call to repentance is: "And still we are not saved!" The return reply? "Repent sinner! Repent!"

Could *the Jew* have repented in Nazi Germany and been saved from the camps? Could *the Negro* have repented and been saved from Jim Crow? Can the malnourished child of the *welfare queen* repent and be saved from hunger tonight?

The answer to these questions should be clear: No. Because there is no repentance possible for those who are essentialized into a social margin not of their own making. These margins are by definition inescapable cultural representations that doom their supposed flesh–and–blood referents to the margins of society.

There is a type of repentance, however, that *is* possible in these situations. The opportunity for repentance is available to all Christian theologians, pastors, and laypeople who have allowed their sincere concern about social sin to be coopted and corrupted by systems of oppression and marginalization. Substantially, this repentance takes the form of receiving those who are despised and marginalized by the type of cultural depictions we have seen and challenging the systems that have so stigmatized them. This repentance does not mean remaining silent about sin in its social dimension. Rather, it means taking a new type of care in the way we talk about and exemplify sin in our particular context. This type of repentance will go far to address the sins of sin–talk. What follows is a way to begin that journey of repentance.

Rules of Engagement:
Constructive Approaches to Sin-Talk

Beyond identifying problematic practices in the sin–talk of some important theologians, I wish to make some positive intervention into the practices of Protestant theologians who write about social sin. Thus far I have only sounded cautionary notes about the dangers that await theologians who attempt to write about social sin without adequately appreciating the discursive economies at work in their contexts. At this point I want to offer constructive comments about appropriate discourse about social sin using the resources that I have identified in the Protestant tradition. Since I have been most concerned about the relationship between discursive economies and the unexamined rhetoric of sin-talk, I will offer my interventions as grammatical and analytic rules of engagement.

Rule 1: Do Not Seek Only Your Own Privilege

The substance of much of my critique of contemporary Protestant sin-talk is that it has not taken seriously enough its tendency to participate in social marginalization. A significant piece of this critique is that theologians in their sin-talk rarely marginalize themselves or their own communities. It is more often the case that they marginalize "others." What goes unspoken is usually this: In their discursive acts that marginalize others, theologians are simultaneously privileging themselves and their communities. It is important to notice this dual character of marginalizing discourse, because it highlights the self-interest that may be involved in our discussions of social sin. This recognition also highlights the validity of the second resource that I drew from the Protestant tradition: Our reflections are never wholly untainted by the sin of our own self-interest.

This rule of engagement points to the reality that the theological formulations of sin-talk that we are most comfortable with are those that render our ecclesial, economic, social positions and perspectives normative. As we saw in Plantinga's work, the more egregious "sinners" we identify in our sin-talk are usually persons and communities whom we had little affinity for in the first place. More often than not, these "sinners" have also been tagged as aberrant by the general customs of society. So, our sin-talk not only reinforces our privilege, but the very structure of society that allows us to hold that privilege. If, as a result of our sin-talk, we and our communities are rendered normative and privileged in relation to others, it is a clear indication that we are perpetuating social sin. We know that we are in trouble when our sin-talk violates the principle of participation by fundamentally denying our mutuality with others in sin and redemption.

Let me make a point about privilege–it is relative! There is no community, no matter what its particular social or economic position, that is safe from the danger of reflecting on sin in a way that profoundly marginalizes others. As has been observed by a number of theologians such as Jacquelyn Grant and Beverly Johnson, even the oppressed can oppress.[5] A noteworthy example of this is the continuing homophobia of the Evangelical African American churches (the Black Church). Here we have a case of members of a community using the very types of biblical interpretation and theological reflection on sin as a tool of oppression that were used against them not many years ago.[6] No one is immune, as Augustine and the reformers reminded us earlier, from talking about the sin of others in a way that minimizes the reality of one's own sin.

Rule 2: Follow the Money: Who Gets Paid?

This second rule is also concerned with the material relationships that are affected by particular theological formulations of sin. By seeking to identify how some enactments of sin-talk direct privilege in certain ways, we are explicitly recognizing that our sin-talk is somehow corrupted by our own implication in sinful systems. Every theologian who writes about sin is prone to some aspect of the sins of sin-talk. What I am contending is not that we can never get it quite right, but that, with care, we might not get it so wrong. It was this lack of care that I critiqued in Plantinga, Niebuhr, and Bonhoeffer.

If the first rule compels us to ask how our sin-talk serves our own self-interest, then this rule admonishes us to ask how others' sin-talk works to their advantage in their context. These two rules invite us to a dialectical posture of humility and suspicion that will not allow us blindly to accept or promulgate enactments of sin-talk that harm other persons and communities. This posture can encourage enough contextual attentiveness to engender more careful language, helping theologians minimize any harmful elements in their sin-talk.

Rule 3: Physician, Heal Yourself!

This rule deals with how the answers to the questions raised by the first two rules might be made meaningful in particular contexts by addressing the actual cultural significations attached to the images, figures, and metaphors we use in our sin-talk. It counsels that we need to ascertain the specific discursive economies at work in our sin-talk. Because the categories that we use to talk about social sin are deeply implicated in the material relations of power in our contexts, we must gain as much clarity as possible about the sensibilities, common sense, and beliefs that are most immediate to us.

Starting from the posture suggested by the first two rules, it is incumbent upon us to ask very definite questions about our contexts. So, using myself as an example, it is important to recognize that I inhabit, minimally, four positions of privilege—I am a male in a largely patriarchal society; I am a first-world resident in a world that has drastic inequities of wealth; I am middle-class in a society that esteems wealth as a sign of God's grace; and I am "straight" in a heterosexist society. The consequence of recognizing these positions of privilege is that I should be keenly aware of the discursive economies that are at work in each of these situations but that may be largely invisible to me given my particular privilege. Thus, if I, as a heterosexual man, were writing about the supposed sinfulness of the "gay lifestyle," I should first ask: Is there any way to be gay and not be a "sinner" in the social or religious context that I inhabit? In other words, is the social identity labeled "gay" rendered in a totally negative way in my context? Based on the terms of "normative" sexuality is it possible, according to common sense, to be at once gay and a faithful Christian? If it is not, why? These types of questions will lead to the sort of material and cultural analysis that may enable me to write about sin in a way that does not immediately reproduce marginalization in my context.

Rule 4: Listen to the "Sinner"

The preceding rules leave out one element of careful sin-talk. What is missing, of course, is the type of engagement that will give us sensitivity to the features of our contexts that reflection in solitude can never do. It is imperative that we incorporate the perspectives of marginalized persons in our sin-talk. With this rule I make explicit use of a method-ological move I first suggested in chapter 1–integrating the testimony of those deemed "sinners" by popular renderings of sin-talk.

This rule also admonishes us to take context and privi-lege seriously. By recognizing that I cannot engage in sin-talk concerning persons who do not hold a similar privilege to mine without importing discursive economies that un-dergird that power differential, I should demonstrate an en-hanced appreciation of the testimony given by persons who are marginalized in my work. Privilege should be given to the testimony of those persons who bear the brunt of social sin in a given context. That is to say, we must explicitly rec-ognize that materially excluded or culturally disdained per-sons and communities are in a far better position to describe how social sin is working in that context than persons who are culturally empowered. By methodologically giving this privilege to the testimony of oppressed persons and com-munities, we significantly enhance the value of our sin-talk. We accomplish an expansion of our vision–the workings of social sin that may be invisible to us are exposed in a way that simple reflection could not attain. Also, this exposure increases the chance that our work will be in solidarity with "the least of these" in any given circumstance.

The Final Statement: Do No Harm!

The interventions that I have outlined above reflect a con-sequentialist approach to sin-talk. As I explained in chapter 1, it is the absence of this concern about consequences that lies behind many of the failures of sin-talk discussed in this book. *Do No Harm* provides the beginning of a method that can help theologians be attentive not only to the ways our sin-talk rearticulates and legitimizes structures of social sin, but also to the consequences of those works. This is a necessary task because our sin-talk should intervene in situations that deny the full humanity of any class or group of persons. Our sin-talk should take seriously its capacity to be a restorative discourse–restoring the humanity of those on the margins of society in public and theological discourse. So, far from being the venue through which marginalization is reiterated, the purpose of our sin-talk should be to challenge and dismantle the discursive economies that participate in and enable marginalization to occur in the first place. Active concern for the way that our sin-talk intervenes in particular cultural contexts can go a long way toward avoiding having our work co-opted by systems of marginalization and exclusion. In the end, a consequentialist approach to sin-talk affirms our conviction that the way we talk about sin in its social dimension matters. It matters because persons hurt by social sin matter.

NOTES

1. The Sins of Sin-Talk

1. Douglas John Hall, "The Political Consequences of Misconceiving Sin," *The Witness* 78 (March 1995): 8.

2. Mary Douglas, *Purity and Danger: An Analysis of the Concepts of Pollution and Taboo* (London: Routledge, 1966), 38–39; chap. 7.

3. Ibid., 51.

4. Ibid., 40.

5. The terms *welfare queen* and *the homosexual* appear in quotation marks to indicate that they have pejorative connotations. Their referents are caricatures, or stereotypes, created as the sum of the discursive economies surrounding these socially conceived figures that do not exist in reality. Other terms that will be used this way include *urban predator, soccer mom, the*

Negro, Negro culture, and *the Jew (der Jude).* In the case of *welfare queen, urban predator,* and *soccer mom,* the objectified people and communities are not specific enough to be caricatures of actual individuals or groups so these terms are no more than fabricated stereotypes (although one can generally guess that they at least signify poor young black men, poor young black women, and middle-class suburban white women, respectively). For the others, however, there are human beings and communities that are being objectified. In order to make the distinctions clear, I will use the following pairs: *the homosexual*/gay person, *the Negro*/African American, *Negro culture*/African American culture, and *the Jew*/Jew. Two terms should be further explained: *gay person* refers to any GLBT (gay, lesbian, bi, or transgendered) person. The term *homosexuality* will generally refer to any nonheterosexual orientation.

6. Lawrence Mead, "The Poverty Debate and Human Nature," in *Welfare in America: Christian Perspectives on a Policy in Crisis,* ed. Stanley W. Carlson-Thies and James W. Skillen (Grand Rapids, Mich.: Eerdmans, 1996), 209–42.

7. Ibid., 211.

8. Ibid., 221.

9. Allan Wallinsky, "The Crisis of Public Order," *The Atlantic Monthly* 276, no. 1 (July 1995): 39–54.

10. In his work *Savage Inequalities: Children in America's Schools* (New York: HarperCollins, 1991), Jonathan Kozol gives an extensive account of the effects of these conditions on urban communities in America. Another work that touches upon the confluence of these events and their undermining effect on the fabric of many urban communities is William Julius Wilson's *When Work Disap-*

pears: The World of the New Urban Poor (New York: Knopf, 1996).

11. Mead, "The Poverty Debate and Human Nature," 231–32 (italics mine).

12. The problem that I have identified is certainly not one confined to the work of contemporary theologians. The trap of the personalization of sins whose implication is patently public has some antiquity. The story of the woman caught in adultery who was about to be stoned in the gospel of John makes this point.

> Jesus went unto the Mount of Olives. And early in the morning he came again into the temple, and all the people came unto him, and he sat down, and taught them. And the scribes and the Pharisees brought unto him a woman taken in adultery; and when they had set her in their midst, They said unto him, Master, this woman was taken in adultery, in the very act. Now Moses in the law commanded us to stone such a woman: but what sayest you? (John 8:1–5)

In the telling of this story, the only thing found worthy–and finally sufficient to condemn the woman to death–was her sin: she had been caught in adultery. We do not know who she was caught with, a man or a woman, or which of them was married and therefore the perpetrator. Neither are we told the circumstances of the adultery. Was she a woman trying to feed her children in a society in which the only commodity that she had was her body, or was she simply the victim of the common human frailty of lust? The point is that in the eyes of the writer, and the stone throwers, the circumstance is beside the point. All that matters is the sin.

13. I am not ignoring the oppression of lesbians that correlates with the marginalization of gay men–this too is a significant problem. Rather, I am recognizing that at least in this portion of contemporary ecclesial contestations the image of the "homosexual" male is dominant. On my read, this has to do with the fact that the debate is going on within a hierarchy that is profoundly patriarchal and consequently oversensitive to men "allowing themselves" to be "used as women." Lesbians in the contemporary context are reserved for another type of demonization–the problem of witchcraft, which has, of course, to do with unnatural power over men.

14. Kenneth O. Gangel, *The Gospel and the Gay* (Nashville: Thomas Nelson, 1978), 166. See also Edward Malloy, *Homosexuality and the Christian Way of Life* (New York: University Press of America, 1981), 168–69, for another example.

15. Paul Ricoeur, *The Symbolism of Evil*, trans. Emerson Buchanan (Boston: Beacon, 1967), 25.

16. Christopher Morse, *Not Every Spirit: A Christian Dogmatics of Disbelief* (Valley Forge, Pa.: Trinity Press International, 1994), 64.

17. Peter Damian, *The Book of Gomorrah: An Eleventh-Century Treatise against Clerical Homosexual Practices*, trans. Pierre J. Payer (Waterloo, Ont.: Wilfred Laurier University Press, 1982), 4.

18. Susan E. Davies, "Oppression and Resurrection Faith," in *The Church with AIDS: Renewal in the Midst of Crisis* (Louisville, Ky.: Westminster John Knox, 1990), 100.

19. Michel Foucault, *The Archaeology of Knowledge and the Discourse on Language* (New York: Pantheon, 1972), parts II and III.

20. Personal conversation.

21. Cornelius Plantinga, *Not the Way It's Supposed to Be: A Breviary of Sin* (Grand Rapids, Mich.: Eerdmans, 1995).

22. Karl A. Menninger, *Whatever Became of Sin?* (New York: Hawthorn, 1973).

23. Ibid., chap. 7; Plantinga, *Not the Way It's Supposed to Be*, chap. 4.

24. Plantinga, *Not the Way It's Supposed to Be*, 7.

25. Dinesh D'Souza, *The End of Racism: Principles for a Multiracial Society* (New York: Free Press, 1995); Richard J. Herrnstein and Charles Murray, *The Bell Curve: Intelligence and Class Structure in American Life* (New York: Free Press, 1994).

26. Here I bring attention to two problematic instances in which Plantinga (*Not the Way It's Supposed to Be*) illustrates his argument using images of predatory urban pathology. First, there is his characterization of "gang rape" as an "urban horror" (65). In this discussion, which Plantinga uses to buttress his claim that context cannot finally account for predatory behavior, he offers absolutely no evidence that gang rape is more prevalent in urban areas or that it is particularly endemic to urban areas. Instead he relies on vague cultural memories of sensational events like the Central Park Jogger rape in New York City (1989). The second instance is Plantinga's description of rap music and its social effects:

> If rap stars publish albums filled with the unlyrical desires to bust vagina walls, to break women's backbones, and to force fellatio on "bitches" till they

"puke," what wreckage might such grunted depravity leave in its wake? How realistic is it to expect fair
and respectful treatment of women by young men
whose stereos, ears, and brains are full of hostile
sexist sludge? How realistic is it to expect from
them, instead, sexual "wilding"–the gang rapes,
bludgeonings, and casual, remorseless murders of
women that startle, and eventually numb, a whole
nation? (71)

Beyond the fact that Plantinga here evidences a
startling ignorance of the genre of musical styles that
may be included in the "rap" category (see Tricia Rose,
*Black Noise: Rap Music and Black Culture in Contemporary
America* [Hanover, N.H.: Wesleyan University Press of
New England, 1994] for a helpful discussion of the genealogy and differences in rap music), his immediate
connection between "gangsta rap" (the proper designation) and "sexual wilding" is unconscionable. With one
stroke of the brush Plantinga misidentifies, mischarac-
terizes, and defames an entire genre of cultural produc-
tion, its audience, and the community from which it
emerges. He does this using as his only evidence–an
editorial by George Will in *Newsweek*: "America's Slide
into the Sewer" (30 [July 1990]: 64). This method of sensational theologizing is possible because Plantinga begins with an assumption about the lethal pathology of
the community in which the criminals live and from
which the music emerges.

2. Created by God, Constructed by Sin

1. Reinhold Niebuhr, *The Nature and Destiny of Man*, vol. 1 (New York: Scribner's, 1941), 17.

2. I will use both of these terms because in Niebuhr's work, while they functionally have the same connotation rhetorically, he reserves the term *primitive* for what we would today call "traditional" or "third-world" cultures, while he utilizes the term *backward* to refer to domestic American nonwhite cultures. My intent in using the terms together is to recognize the kinship that Niebuhr presumed to exist between all nonwhite cultures. Also, during Niebuhr's career he changed from using the term *egoism* to using *egotism*. This change does not seem to have signaled a substantive alteration of his intent, but rather the evolution of language. Throughout this chapter I will use the terms interchangeably, shifting only to mirror Niebuhr's usage in the text under immediate consideration.

3. Niebuhr, *The Nature and Destiny of Man*, chap. 3.

4. Reinhold Niebuhr, *The Irony of American History* (New York: Scribner's, 1952), 126. I am presuming that by "national kinship" Niebuhr has in mind the "modern" idea of society as a confederation of individuals bound together by some common commitment. This being opposed, of course, to the idea of allegiance to some sense of primordial attachment. (See Stuart Geertz, *The Interpretation of Cultures: Selected Essays* [New York: Basic, 1973], chap. 10, for a helpful discussion of the difference between civic relationships and blood relations among people).

5. Reinhold Niebuhr, *The Self and the Dramas of History* (New York: Scribner's, 1955), 18.
6. Niebuhr, *The Nature and Destiny of Man*, 41–42.
7. Ibid., 179.
8. This particular formulation–the "Negro Problem"–was the pervasive language used to delineate the social and political place of African Americans during much of the first half of the twentieth century. Beyond being a simple linguistic formulation, this phrasing represents the cultural prism through which the Negro was interpreted. That prism saw the Negro as a problem for society that must be solved. The pervasiveness of this interpretation is evident in the range of literature that took "the problem" as being gainsaid. Some examples of that literature are: Benjamin Brawley, *A Social History of the American Negro: Being a History of the Negro Problem in the United States* (New York: Macmillan, 1921); Gunnar Myrdal, *An American Dilemma: The Negro Problem and Modern Democracy* (New York: Harper, 1944); Edgar T. Thompson, ed., *Race Relations and the Race Problem: A Definition and an Analysis* (Durham, N.C.: Duke University Press, 1939).
9. Niebuhr, *The Self and the Dramas of History*, 41.
10. Niebuhr, *The Nature and Destiny of Man*, 162–63.
11. Paul Tillich, *Systematic Theology*, vol. 2, (Chicago: The University of Chicago Press 1957), 29–44.
12. Niebuhr, *The Self and the Dramas of History*, part II.
13. "In short, we are confronted with evidence that the thesis of Biblical faith, that the self is in dialogue with a God who must be defined as a 'person' because He embodies both the structure of being and a transcendent

freedom, is more valid than the alternative theses which find much greater favor among the sophisticated." Ibid., 71.

14. Ibid., 4.

15. Ibid.

16. Ibid., 30–33.

17. Ibid.

18. While certainly this schema seems a bit naive in relation to what we know as a society about human development, it is the framework within which Niebuhr was working; so we will accept it here for the sake of argument.

19. Niebuhr, *The Nature and Destiny of Man*, 179.

20. Ibid., 186.

21. Ibid., 57–61.

22. Ibid., 57–58.

23. Reinhold Niebuhr, *Moral Man and Immoral Society* (New York: Scribner's, 1932), 21–22.

24. Ibid., chap. 5.

25. Niebuhr, *The Nature and Destiny of Man*, 74.

26. Niebuhr uses these terms interchangeably. To ensure continuity, I will use the term *collectivism* throughout this chapter.

27. Niebuhr, *The Nature and Destiny of Man*, 69.

28. Ibid., 68.

29. Ibid., 70.

30. Ibid., 68–69.

31. Reinhold Niebuhr, *The Godly and the Ungodly; Essays on the Religious and Secular Dimensions of Modern Life* (London: Faber & Faber Limited, 1958), chap. 4.

32. Ibid., 78.

33. I do not mean to invoke the images of the organized racists of Niebuhr's era (e.g., White Citizens Councils), rather, I mean to speak about the entire system of racial privilege that underlies the identity of whiteness during his era. The following works are representative of those written in Niebuhr's era: Oliver C. Cox, *Class and Race: A Study in Social Dynamics* (Garden City, N.Y.: Doubleday, 1948); Bertram W. Doyle, *The Etiquette of Race Relations in the South: A Study in Social Control* (Chicago: The University of Chicago Press, 1937); Charles S. Johnson, *Patterns of Negro Segregation* (New York: Harper, 1943); Karl Manheim, *Ideology and Utopia* (New York: Harcourt & Brace, 1936); Herbert A. Miller, "Race and Class Parallelism," *Annals of the American Academy of Political and Social Science* 140 (November 1928): 1–5; W. Lloyd Warner, "American Caste and Class," *American Journal of Sociology* 42 (September 1936): 234–37.

34. Niebuhr, *The Godly and the Ungodly*, 81: "Prejudice may of course be any opinion with which we do not agree. Race prejudice may best be defined, however, as primarily group pride, which is almost always an extension of the survival impulse of the group."

35. Ibid.

36. Myrdal, *An American Dilemma*. We find Niebuhr's paean to this work in his essay "Tribalism and Inhumanity," in *The Godly and the Ungodly*, 99; see also Niebuhr's review of *An American Dilemma*, by Gunnar Myrdal, *Christianity and Society* 9, no. 3 (summer 1994): 42.

37. Myrdal, *An American Dilemma*, 929–30.

38. Ibid.

39. Ibid., 927. While spread out over more than a decade, the following works come to the same sort of culturally and racially biased conclusion as Myrdal: Guy B. Johnson, "The Negro and Crime," *Annals of the American Academy of Political and Social Science* 217 (September 1941): 299–304; Abram Kardiner and Lionel Ovesey, *The Mark of Oppression: Explorations in the Personality of the American Negro* (New York: Norton, 1951); Earl R. Moses, "Community Factors in Negro Delinquency," *Journal of Negro Education* 5 (April 1936): 220–27. In making note of the literature about the "pathology of the Negro community" I in no way want to legitimate its claims. Rather, I want to demonstrate how widespread this cultural assumption was in Niebuhr's context.

40. Niebuhr, *The Godly and the Ungodly,* 78–79.

41. Reinhold Niebuhr, "School, Church, and the Ordeals of Integration," *Christianity and Crisis* 16, no. 16 (October 1956): 121–22; "Man, the Unregenerate Tribalist," *Christianity and Crisis* 24, no. 12 (July 6, 1964): 133–34.

42. W. E. B. Du Bois and Augustus Granville Dill, eds., *Morals and Manner among Negro Americans* (Atlanta: Atlanta University Press, 1914); Willis D. Weatherford, *Present Forces in Negro Progress* (New York: Association Press, 1912); Willis D. Weatherford and Charles S. Johnson, *Race Relations: Adjustment of Whites and Negroes in the United States* (Boston: D. C. Heath, 1934); Melville J. Herskovits, *The Myth of the Negro Past* (New York: Harper, 1941).

43. Reinhold Niebuhr, *Love and Justice: Selections from the Shorter Writings of Reinhold Niebuhr,* ed. D. B. Robertson (Philadelphia: Westminster, 1957), 127.

3. Difference as Defilement

1. The framework that I am specifically using is that men-
    tioned in chapter 1: Paul Ricoeur, in *The Symbolism of Evil*,
    trans. Emerson Buchanan (Boston: Beacon, 1967), con-
    tends that the association between sin and defilement
    is a tight one, so, when one talks about defilement and
    purity, sin is the subtext invoked.

2. The term *Jewish difference* refers to the idea that the Jew-
    ish people were in some immutable way different from
    other Europeans. While this particularity was mediated
    in varying ways (e.g., racially and/or culturally), it was
    always deemed to have some metaphysical origin and
    significance.

3. This legislation specifically disqualified persons with
    more than one-quarter Jewish ancestry from holding
    offices within the civil service. This exclusion extended
    to church appointments as well because of the config-
    uration of the relationship between the German Protes-
    tant Church and the German government. Because the
    church was an arm of the civil service, positions such as
    pastor or bishop were state sanctioned.

4. Some statement of chronology is necessary. Bonhoef-
    fer's response was immediately addressed to the civil
    service "restoration" acts. These acts were passed a
    number of months before the infamous Brown Synod
    of September 1933. This point is crucial because it
    places Bonhoeffer's essay squarely at the forefront of
    the prophetic Christian response to the Nazi persecu-
    tion of Germany's Jewish citizenry. This is further ex-
    emplified by Bonhoeffer's refusal to sign the main body
    of the Bethel Confession, a document upon which he

had labored, because it did not deal forthrightly with the issue of Jewish persecution. It should additionally be noted that these documents predated the more famous Barmen Declaration by nearly a year. I emphasize these points because in my estimation they contextualize Bonhoeffer's challenge to the German government's persecution of the Jews: It was early and it was extraordinary.

5. I am not ignoring the insights of linguistic and social theorists (e.g., Michel Foucault), who correctly point to the notion that social discourse is by nature value laden. I am more interested in the fact that in Bonhoeffer's context, there was no need to interrogate the discourse for its subterranean meaning. In the context of the nascent era of the Nazi regime in Germany, the rhetorical assault on the Jews was right out in the open, so to speak. This observation is made by historians such as Daniel Jonah Goldhagen, *Hitler's Willing Executioners: Ordinary Germans and the Holocaust* (New York: Vintage, 1997), as well as by literary theorists such as Kenneth Burke, "The Rhetoric of Hitler's 'Battle,'" in *The Philosophy of Literary Form* (Chicago: University of Chicago Press 1973), 191–220 (reprinted from *Let My People Go: Some Practical Proposals for Dealing with Hitler's Massacre of the Jews and an Appeal to the British Public*, ed. Victor Gollancz [London: Gollancz, 1943]).

6. From this point on I will use the term *the Jew* to denote the cultural figure, and *Jew* in those instances when I am referring to actual Jewish persons or communities.

7. My use of the term *vocation* draws, again, on the work of Ricoeur. In his framework, defilement is not a contamination that happens as a result of a particular set of

actions. Rather, defilement is brought about because the very being of the agent who defiles bears an ontological uncleanness. The propensity of the defiling agent to bring about contamination is therefore a part of the very terms of it existence (Ricoeur, *The Symbolism of Evil*, 25). See also Mary Douglas, *Purity and Danger: An Analysis of the Concepts of Pollution and Taboo* (London: Routledge, 1966), esp. chaps. 1 and 2.

8. The term *Jewish Question* functioned in the German cultural context in much the same way that *Negro Problem* functioned in the American context. The phrase encapsulated a cultural common sense that the place of Jewish persons and their communities was continually an open question, and one that presented somewhat of a conundrum for German society. See John Weiss, *Ideology of Death: Why the Holocaust Happened in Germany* (Chicago: Ivan R. Dee, 1996).

9. Michael Burleigh and Wolfgang Wipperman, *The Racial State: Germany 1933–1945* (Cambridge: Cambridge University Press, 1991), chaps. 2–3.

10. For a helpful synopsis of the evolution of the Aryan mythos, see Jacques Barzun's *Race: A Study in Superstition* (New York: Harper & Row, 1963).

11. Saul Friedländer, *The Years of Persecution, 1933–1939*, vol. 1 of *Nazi Germany and the Jew* (New York: HarperCollins, 1997), chap. 2.

12. Ibid., 31–137. These terms, *Volk* and *völkisch*, might be defined simply as "people" or "folk," meaning a particular self-identified group. In the context of Nazi Germany the words had a very specific meaning. They were used to connote the "particular spiritual or characterological

factors living in" the German people that became apparent "in its creativity and its history." Nathan Roten-
streich, *Jews and German Philosophy: The Polemics of
Emancipation* (New York: Shocken, 1984), 147.

13. Robert P. Ericksen and Susannah Heschel, eds., *Betrayal:
German Churches and the Holocaust* (Minneapolis: Fortress
Press, 1999), 9–14.

14. Norman Rich, *Hitler's War Aims: Ideology, the Nazi State, and
the Course of Expansion* (New York: Norton, 1973), 13.

15. Orlando Patterson, *Slavery and Social Death: A Comparative
Study* (Cambridge: Harvard University Press, 1982),
chap. 1.

16. According to Kenneth Burke, materialization is the creation of a material reference, some aspect of material
reality, upon which the notion of the people may be an-
chored. This identification of a material reference is the
symbolic rendering of the social order as a living thing–
an inanimate principle is hardly the stuff new worlds
are made of. This is most often accomplished through
the deployment of linguistic figures having to do with
the forces that animate living beings (e.g., blood and
spirit). Thus, the idea of a people of a particular race, or
a certain sort of blood, becomes the predicate of the nation. Likewise, the ideals that are "embodied" within the
society are not rendered as political ideologies that
have gained wide acceptance, but are rather portrayed
as emblematic of the spirit of the people who make up
the society. What had previously been an abstract ideal
becomes rooted within material reality. "The Rhetoric of
Hitler's Battle," in *The Philosophy of Literary Form*, 191–220;
reprinted from Gollancz, *Let My People Go*.

17. In recent decades the notion of the other has been interrogated by several disciplines: philosophy, anthropology, sociology, and theology. What this has helped to clarify is the role that "the other" plays in the construction of communal identity within the discourse of a particular society. That is, these analyses have pointed to the ways that assigning pariah status to those groups who are structurally designated "other" has functioned in both the coalescence of communal identity and the ritualized amelioration of internal conflict within the community. Albert Memmi, *The Colonizer and the Colonized*, trans. Howard Greenfeld (Boston: Beacon, 1991).

18. Dan Cohn-Sherbok, *The Crucified Jew: Twenty Centuries of Christian Anti-Semitism* (Grand Rapids, Mich.: Eerdmans, 1992).

19. Dietrich Bonhoeffer, *No Rusty Swords; Letters, Lectures and Notes 1928–1936*, ed. Edwin H. Robertson, trans. Edwin H. Robertson and John Bowden (New York: Harper & Row, 1965), 221.

20. Ibid., 222.

21. Kenneth Barnes, "Dietrich Bonhoeffer and Hitler's Persecution of the Jews," in Ericksen and Heschel, *Betrayal*, 114–15.

22. Augustine, *Concerning the City of God against the Pagans*, ed. Henry Bettenson (New York: Penguin, 1972).

23. Martin Luther "Secular Authority: To What Extent It Should Be Obeyed," in *Martin Luther: Selections from His Writings*, ed. John Dillenberger (New York: Doubleday 1961), 363–402.

24. Bonhoeffer, *No Rusty Swords*, 225.

25. Ibid., 227.

26. Ibid., italics mine.

27. Robert P. Ericksen, *Theologians under Hitler: Gerhard Kittel, Paul Althaus, and Emanuel Hirsch* (New Haven: Yale University Press, 1985).

28. Bonhoeffer, *No Rusty Swords*, 227.

29. Ibid, 226.

30. Ibid.

31. Geffrey B. Kelly and F. Burton Nelson, eds., *A Testament to Freedom: The Essential Writings of Dietrich Bonhoeffer* (San Francisco: HarperSanFrancisco, 1990), 16. I do not mean at all to suggest that Bonhoeffer intended this reading. Rather, I want to make clear several instances where his unselfconscious acceptance of the discursive economies embedded in his discussion of the "Jewish problem" undercut the section of his essay on the "baptized Jew."

32. In Bonhoeffer's context the word *racist* did not have the same implication that it does in contemporary discourse. The Jews were understood to be a different race from the majority of the population even though the vast majority of Jews were physically indistinguishable from other Germans. Thus, the categories of pigmentation and language that attend much of the contemporary discourses about race were not explicitly at work in Bonhoeffer's context. For a fuller explication of the way that race did function in that context, see Juan Comas, "Racial Myths," in *The Race Question in Modern Society* (New York: UNESCO, 1961).

33. The *Glaubenbewegung "Deutsche Christen"* was the primary *völkish* movement that functioned in the Christian community, particularly the German Protestant Church, during the Nazi era. It was a political/ecclesial movement that sought to synthesize Christian proclamation and teaching with Nazi ideology. An important tenet of

this movement was the dejudaization of Christianity, by a reinterpretation of the Bible and a racial cleansing of the church. The movement gained significant power after the infamous "Brown Synod," in July 1933 where supporters of the Nazi regime were elected to every important office of the German Protestant Church. See Doris L. Bergen, "Storm Troopers of Christ: The German Christian Movement and the Ecclesial Final Solution," in Ericksen and Heschel, *Betrayal*, 40–47; see also Doris Bergen, *Twisted Cross: The German Christian Movement in the Third Reich* (Chapel Hill, N.C.: University of North Carolina Press, 1996).

34. Bonhoeffer, *No Rusty Swords*, 227.

35. Ibid.

36. "Thus from the point of view of the church it is not baptized Christians of Jewish race who are Jewish Christians; in the church's view the Jewish Christian is the man who lets membership of the people of God, of the church of Christ, be determined by the observance of a divine law [e.g., the racial unity of members in the community]. In contrast, the Gentile Christian knows no presupposition for membership of the people of God, the church of Christ, but the call of God by his Word in Christ" (Bonhoeffer, *No Rusty Swords*, 228).

37. Étienne Balibar and Immanuel Wallerstein, *Race, Nation, Class: Ambiguous Identities*, trans. Christ Turner (New York: Verso, 1991).

38. Ibid, 17.

39. Ibid., 17–18.

40. Ibid., 22.

41. Ibid., 24.

42. These were the people of a small French town who, at great risk to themselves and their town, hid their Jewish neighbors from the Nazi and Vichy authorities lest they perish. See Phillip Paul Haille, *Lest Innocent Blood Be Shed: The Story of the Village of Le Chambon, and How Goodness Happened There* (New York: Harper & Row, 1979).

4. Wisdom from the Tradition

1. Max Weber, *The Protestant Ethic and the Spirit of Capitalism,* trans. Talcott Parsons (New York: Scribner's, 1930).

2. Ernst Troeltsch, *The Social Teaching of the Christian Churches,* 2 vols., trans. Olive Wyon (Louisville, Ky.: Westminster John Knox Press, 1992); *Protestantism and Progress: The Significance of Protestantism for the Rise of the Modern World,* trans. W. Montgomery (Philadelphia: Fortress Press, 1986).

3. I am referring to the idea that Troeltsch identifies in Luther's theology that the particular place a person inhabits in the socioeconomic order of his or her society is ordained by God and the fulfillment of the expectations associated with that status should consequently be interpreted as a "calling." Implicit in this conception is, of course, a fundamental acceptance of the particular political, social, and economic relationships that one finds oneself born into, meaning that the truly religious life is not one that transcends the social order in a prophetic manner, but rather one that assumes a posture of seeing God's plan in any given social arrangement. Troeltsch, *The Social Teaching of the Christian Churches,* vol. 2, 528–44.

Troeltsch understood the Calvinist ethos to be an ethic that was "a current–definite, particularly powerful, and influential–of the bourgeois way of life in general. This was the predominance of labor and of the 'calling,' of industry for its own sake, a process of objectifying work and the results of work" (646). The result of this current of thought was that in the end Calvinism maintained a conviction that material prosperity in itself was virtuous and a sign of God's election.

4. R. H. Tawney, *Religion and the Rise of Capitalism: A Historical Study* (New York: Harcourt, Brace, 1926).

5. Ibid., 72–74, 96–97.

6. Notable in their dissension from Weber's thesis are Werner Sombart in "The Role of Religion in the Formation of the Capitalist Spirit," Winthrop S. Hudson in "Puritanism and the Spirit of Capitalism," and H. M. Robertson in "A Criticism of Max Weber and His School." All of these essays are found in the volume *Protestantism and Capitalism: The Weber Thesis and Its Critics*, ed. Robert W. Green (Boston: D. C. Heath and Company, 1959).

7. Reinhold Niebuhr, *Moral Man and Immoral Society* (New York: Scribner's, 1932), 80. Niebuhr gives fuller exposition of this point in chapter 5. The description he provides of the relationship between the privileged classes and religion is very similar to that offered by Weber and Troeltsch.

8. Ibid., 8–9.

9. Henri Rondet, *Original Sin: The Patristic and Theological Background*, trans. Cajetan Finegan (New York: Alba House, 1972), chaps. 1–4.

10. Augustine, *Concerning the City of God against the Pagans*, trans. Henry Bettenson (London: Penguin, 1972), book

13, chap. 3; "The Punishment and Forgiveness of Sins" and "The Baptism of Little Ones," in *Answer to the Pelagians I*, vol. I/23 of *The Works of Saint Augustine*, ed. John E. Rotelle, trans. Roland J. Teske (Hyde Park, N. Y.: New City Press, 1997), book 1, paragraphs 2–21; *The Retractions*, vol. 60 of *Fathers of the Church*, trans. Mary Inez Bogan (Washington, D.C.: Catholic University of America Press, 1968), chap. 14, paragraph 3.

11. Augustine, "The Punishment and Forgiveness of Sins," book 1, paragraphs 7–11.

12. Martin Luther, *Bondage of the Will*, trans. J. I. Packer and O. R. Johnson (Westwood, N.J.: Fleming Revell, 1957), 298.

13. John Calvin, *The Institutes of the Christian Faith*, ed. T. McNeill, trans. Ford Lewis Battles (Philadelphia: Westminster, 1960), book 1, chap. 1, article 1.

14. Augustine, "The Grace of Christ and Original Sin," in *Answer to the Pelagians I* vol. I/23, of *The Works of Saint Augustine*, 458.

15. Martin Luther, *What Luther Says: An Anthology*, ed. Ewald M. Plass (Saint Louis, Mo.: Concordia, 1959), 1295–96.

16. Martin Luther, *Commentary on Genesis*, trans. J. Theodore Mueller (Grand Rapids, Mich.: Zondervan, 1958), 63.

17. Martin Luther, *Works*, vol. 25, trans. Hilton C. Oswald (St. Louis, Mo.: Concordia, 1972), 296–302.

18. John Calvin, *Commentary on the Epistle of Paul the Apostle to the Romans*, trans., John Owen (Grand Rapids, Mich.: Baker, 1979).

19. John Calvin, *Institutes of the Christian Religion*, ed. John T. McNeill, trans. Ford Lewis Battles (Philadelphia: Westminster, 1960) (C.I. II.i.6).

20. I am not unmindful of the heritage of the Christian tradition in identifying the "sin of the Jews" as being

distinctive—works such as Dan Cohn-Sherbok's *The Crucified Jew: Twenty Centuries of Christian Anti-Semitism* (Grand Rapids, Mich.: Eerdmans, 1992) give ample evidence of its longevity. Nor, for that matter am I oblivious to Calvin's participation in his culture's anti-Semitism. Rather, I am suggesting that it is possible to appropriate a reading of Calvin that recognizes this hereditary tendency and to work actively to subvert it.

21. An important example of this use of the idea is the perennial cultural discussion about the relative place of African Americans in American society. The number of sociological, anthropological, and theological works throughout the nineteenth and twentieth centuries that have tried to rationalize the marginalized place of African American, in the civic life of the United States is legion. Works that give an incisive account of this literature are Thomas F. Gossett's *Race: The History of an Idea in America* (New York: Oxford University Press, 1997) and Barbara Jeanne Fields's article "Slavery, Race and Ideology in the United States of America," *New Left Review* 181 (May/June 1990): 95–118.

22. Augustine, *On Free Choice of the Will*, trans. Anna S. Benjamin and L. H. Hackstaff (Indianapolis: Bobbs-Merrill, 1964), 155.

23. Martin Luther, *Bondage of the Will*, 107.

24. I do not mean that all theologians exemplify the type of arrogance I have critiqued in their sin-talk. The works of feminist and womanist theologians serve as forceful reminders of the folly of such blanket claims. What I do contend, however, is that at best a theologian can have a vantage point to see social sin—we can never

see it in its entirety. The belief that we can see sin in its entirety is a danger for every theologian, marginalized or mainstream. This is what I am calling "arrogant."

5. Redeeming Sin-Talk

1. Georg Friedrich Hegel, *Philosophy of the Right*, trans. T. M. Knox (Oxford: Oxford University Press, 1967), 20–30; Reinhold Niebuhr, *The Nature and Destiny of Man* (New York: Scribner's, 1941), 54–65.
2. Niebuhr, *The Nature and Destiny of Man*, 57–58.
3. Christoph Schwöbel, "Imago Liberatis: Human and Divine Freedom," in *God and Freedom: Essays in Historical and Systematic Theology*, ed. Colin E. Gunton (Edinburgh: T. & T. Clark, 1995), 57–81.
4. Colin E. Gunton, "God, Grace and Freedom," in *God and Freedom: Essays in Historical and Systematic Theology*, ed. Colin E. Gunton (Edinburgh: T. & T. Clark, 1995), 119–33.
5. Jacquelyn Grant, *White Women's Christ and Black Women's Jesus: Feminist Christology and Womanist Response* (Atlanta: Scholars, 1989), chap. 7; Elizabeth A. Johnson, *She Who Is: The Mystery of God in Feminist Theological Discourse* (New York: Crossroad, 1992), 28.
6. Gary David Comstock has collected a number of essays by preachers and theologians about the issue of the Black Church and gays and lesbians in a helpful volume titled *A Whosoever Church: Welcoming Lesbians and Gay Men into African American Congregations* (Louisville, Ky.: Westminster John Knox, 2001).

SELECTED BIBLIOGRAPHY

These works were not cited in the book but were nonetheless important to my thinking about the subjects covered in the text.

Browning, Christopher R. *The Path to Genocide: Essays on Launching the Final Solution.* Cambridge: Cambridge University Press, 1992.

Des Pres, Terrence. *The Survivor: An Anatomy of Life in the Death Camps.* New York: Oxford University Press, 1976.

Engel, Mary Potter. "Evil, Sin, and Violation of the Vulnerable." In *Lift Every Voice: Constructing Christian Theologies from the Underside.* Edited by Susan Brooks Thistlethwaite and Mary Potter Engel. San Francisco: HarperCollins, 1990.

Farley, Wendy. *Tragic Vision and Divine Compassion: A Contemporary Theodicy.* Louisville, Ky.: Westminster John Knox, 1990.

Geertz, Clifford. *The Interpretation of Cultures.* New York: Basic, 1973.

Goldhagen, Daniel Jonah. *Hitler's Willing Executioners: Ordinary Germans and the Holocaust.* New York: Random House, 1997.

Gordon, Lewis R., ed. *Existence in Black: An Anthology of Black Existential Philosophy.* New York: Routledge, 1997.

Gossett, Thomas F. *Race: The History of an Idea in America.* New York: Oxford University Press, 1997.

Hale, Grace Elizabeth. *Making Whiteness: The Culture of Segregation in the South 1890–1940.* New York: Vintage, 1998.

Harris, Cheryl I. "Whiteness as Property" *Harvard Law Review* 106 (1993): 1709–95, particularly 1710–12.

Hunter, James Davison. *Culture Wars: The Struggle to Define America.* San Francisco: Basic, 1991.

———. *Before the Shooting Starts: Searching for Democracy in America's Culture War.* New York: Free Press, 1994.

Lewis, David L. *W.E.B. Du Bois: A Reader.* New York: Henry Holt, 1995.

McFarland, Ian A. *Listening to the Least: Doing Theology from the Outside In.* Cleveland, Ohio: United Church Press, 1998.

Marsh, Charles. *Reclaiming Dietrich Bonhoeffer: The Promise of His Theology.* New York: Oxford University Press, 1994.

Nelson, Susan L. (Dunfee). "The Sin of Hiding: A Feminist Critique of Reinhold Niebuhr's Sin of Pride." *Soundings* 65 (fall 1982): 316–27.

Park, Andrew Sung, and Susan L. Nelson, eds. *The Other Side of Sin: Woundedness from the Perspective of the Sinned-Against.* Albany: State University of New York Press, 2001.

Peck, William J. "From Cain to the Death Camps: An Essay on Bonhoeffer and Judaism" *Union Seminary Quarterly Review* 28 (winter 1973): 158–76.

Rubenstein, Betty Rogers, and Michael Berenbaum. *What Kind of God?: Essays in Honor of Richard L. Rubenstein.* Studies in the Shoah, vol. 11. Lanham, Md.: University Press of America, 1995.

Said, Edward W. *Orientalism.* New York: Vintage, 1979.

Snyder, T. Richard. *The Protestant Ethic and the Spirit of Punishment.* Grand Rapids, Mich.: Eerdmans, 2001.

Stringfellow, William. *A Keeper of the Word: Selected Writings of William Stringfellow.* Edited by Bill Wylie Kellermann. Grand Rapids, Mich.: Eerdmans, 1994.

Suchocki, Marjorie. *The Fall to Violence: Original Sin in Relational Theology.* New York: Continuum, 1995.

Thurman, Howard. *Jesus and the Disinherited.* Richmond, Ind.: Friends United Press, 1981.

Toole, David. *Waiting for Godot in Sarajevo: Theological Reflections on Nihilism, Tragedy, and Apocalypse.* Boulder, Colo.: Westview, 1998.

Weaver, Jace. "Original Simplicities and Original Complexities: Reinhold Niebuhr, Ethnocentrism, and the Myth of American Exceptionalism." *Journal of the American Academy of Religion* 63, no. 2 (summer 1995): 231–48.

Weiss, John. *Ideology of Death: Why the Holocaust Happened in Germany.* Chicago: Ivan R. Dee, 1996.

West, Cornel. *Keeping Faith: Philosophy and Race in America.* New York: Routledge, 1993.

Williams, Mary E., ed. *Culture Wars: Opposing Viewpoints.* San Diego: Greenhaven, 1999.

Williams, Robert R., ed. *Theology and the Interhuman: Essays in Honor of Edward Farley*. Valley Forge, Pa.: Trinity Press International, 1995.

Young, Josiah Ulysses, III. *No Difference in the Fare: Dietrich Bonhoeffer and the Problem of Racism*. Grand Rapids, Mich.: Eerdmans, 1998.